25 Basic
Bible Studies

25 Basic Bible Studies

INCLUDING

TWO CONTENTS

TWO REALITIES

Francis A. Schaeffer

Foreword by
Udo W. Middelmann

CROSSWAY BOOKS • WHEATON, ILLINOIS
A DIVISION OF GOOD NEWS PUBLISHERS

First printing, 1996

Printed in the United States of America

Library of Congress Cataloging-in-Publication Data
Schaeffer, Francis A. (Francis August)
    [Basic Bible studies]
    25 basic Bible studies ; with, Two contents, two realities /
Francis Schaeffer.
        p.   cm.
    First work originally published : Basic Bible studies. Wheaton,
Ill. : Tyndale House Publishers, 1972. 2nd work originally
published : London : Hodder and Stoughton, c1974.
    ISBN 0-89107-893-2
    1. Bible—Textbooks..   2. Theology, Doctrinal—Popular works.
3. Apologetics.   I. Schaeffer, Francis A. (Francis August). Two
contents, two realities. II. Title. III. Title: Two contents, two
realities.
BS605.2.S3 1996
220'.02'02—dc20
                                   95-49080

04		03		02		01		00		99		98		97		96
15	14	13	12	11	10	9	8	7	6	5	4	3	2	1

C O N T E N T S

PART ONE

Basic Bible Studies

SECTION FOUR: THINGS OF THE FUTURE

PART TWO

Two Contents, Two Realities

PART

ONE

Basic Bible Studies

FOREWORD

You probably know someone like Dr. Otten—a family doctor with a very busy life of house calls and hospital visits. His was a life interrupted by interruptions. Summer and winter he would drive at great speed up and down the narrow Swiss valleys, dotted with villages and isolated farms, in response to medical emergencies.

At times he would stay on after attending to the family, to discuss real questions about life and death. He was a man with more than clinical interests, a man with a wider education than what is characteristic of a backward mountain valley. Like many modern people, he had not been exposed to Christianity—except on a superficial religious level, which rarely interests an educated person with questions to be answered.

Francis Schaeffer's *Twenty-five Basic Bible Studies* were first written for Dr. Otten in the early 1950s to help him understand the simple and obvious teaching of the Bible. Later they were translated into German, Italian, and Dutch and copied on an old Gestetner mimeograph. Before long they became a small booklet that could be handed to anyone who wanted to know more about the teachings of Christianity.

Dr. Otten was too busy to read the whole Bible. Perhaps also the stories, poetry, and history of the Bible were alien to him. Yet he wanted to know what the Bible taught. He wanted to understand the worldview or the system of thought presented in it.

I too first came into contact with Christianity through this booklet. I had assumed that faith stands in contrast to understanding and that Christianity, therefore, is only for the person with "religious needs." But when I opened *Twenty-five Basic Bible Studies*, I found to my surprise a structured presentation of what the Bible teaches. The studies covered the various themes I had associated with Christianity, but about which I had no clear notion. I pored over the chapters night after night, only to discover that there was order, coherence, and verification to the Bible. Rather than a vague quest to find God, I found a comprehensive explanation of the kind of universe we live in as human beings.

The studies before you are not intended to be read for the "personal meaning" they may have for the reader. Instead, Dr. Schaeffer gathered the Bible passages in each chapter around a given theme, in order to delineate the biblical view of the world. Different chapters, for example, present what the Bible says about God and man, about reality and false views, about sin and redemption, about history and our own responsibilities. As the passages in each chapter are studied, the basic philosophical and personal questions that men and women have raised for millennia are answered from the Bible.

The studies are addressed to the person who is not interested in simply "being religious," but who wants to *know* what the Bible teaches. They bring the Bible to the marketplace of ideas, so that anyone can weigh the evidence and discover whether the content of the Bible speaks about the real world, real people, real problems, and real solutions, and whether it is therefore accurate and credible.

This form of presenting Christianity reflects Dr. Schaeffer's own mind. But it has also been a central part of the work of L'Abri—a place where people knew they could receive answers to the questions they raise openly, fearlessly, and with integrity. For Dr. Schaeffer, the truth of Christianity was not an "assumption," nor a matter of blind "faith." "There is only one reason to be a Christian," he would frequently say to the thousands who came through the years, "and that is that Christianity is true to reality. It is 'true' Truth." By this play on words he wanted to counter the existentialist and now postmodern suggestion that all truth is merely "personal truth"—merely a personal story or a personal experience in faith, rather than something absolute and eternal.

Neither Dr. Otten nor Dr. Schaeffer would have become Christians with such a set of assumptions. They were people who insisted on something different, on something real. They wanted to know how to understand the real world of things and ideas, of personal beings and purpose, how to live in the world while being honest with the beauty and tragedy of a natural world and human existence.

When you start your study of the chapters in this book, you will be taken back to the beginning of all questions: What is eternal? Do we live in a universe with personality, or is everything part of a cosmic machine? Is God good, evil, or indifferent? How can we know anything? These and additional subjects would later be treated by Dr. Schaeffer in greater length in *He Is There and He Is Not Silent* and other books. In fact, the systematic gathering of biblical information found in these Bible studies are the foundation for all of Schaeffer's thought and work.

The Bible is not a religious book—at least not in the sense of religion being an effort to link one's life to a private world of meaning or to resign oneself to fate. In the Bible, as these studies show, we are confronted with propositions about the world we live in, which we can examine in light of our observations and determine whether they are true, fitting, and unique. We are brought into a situation where a true meeting of the minds takes place—as the creature acknowledges with his whole being the existence of the God of the Bible. And if, through the study of these chapters, this is your own response, you are then encouraged to bow before Him both *intellectually* as a creature and *morally* as a sinner, and thus to receive in the work of the historic Christ your own moral forgiveness and hope for eternal life.

Dr. Schaeffer's own intellectual and spiritual development finds expression in these studies as well. He was not born into a family of Christians. He set out to reject what he knew of Christianity, but decided to read through the Bible once before he did so. But as he started to read, he discovered that the Bible in its propositions and descriptions addressed the foundational questions of existence—whether as stated formally by the great philosophers in every age or as commonly discussed by the man in the street. The Bible, Schaeffer discovered, gave real and coherent answers in a structured, systematic way.

You will be pleased by the simplicity of the studies. They are structured so that a verse or passage of Scripture is given with a very brief explanation. It is helpful to read the verses found before and after the given reference to discover the context. With each passage bearing on the specific subject under discussion, the general approach is to ask, "What does the Bible say about . . . ?"

As you fill out the pieces of the puzzle, you will be surprised by the view of the whole—a view that reveals a new and real world of meaning, beauty, and moral direction. You will discover that Christianity requires acknowledgment by the whole person—with mind and feelings—and that there are not individual truths with personal religious meaning, but only *the* Truth of the universe as given in the Bible. And when we bow before the God who makes Himself known to us in the language of the Bible and in the Christ of history, He removes the moral and intellectual foolishness of sin from us and wonderfully gives to us eternal life.

Udo W. Middelmann, President
The Francis A. Schaeffer Foundation
August 1995

INTRODUCTION

These twenty-five basic Bible studies are meant to give an understanding of the whole system of teaching given in the Bible. Very often when people begin to study the Scripture, they do not see the relationship of all its parts. However, because one of the wonderful things about the Bible is its unity, Bible study without keeping this unity in mind is a real loss.

Thus, each individual lesson should be studied with the whole table of contents consciously in mind, so that each lesson can be seen in relationship to the whole Bible's teaching.

These twenty-five studies are not meant to be read as a book. If they were, a much more detailed text would have been given. Rather, they are to be followed to be a help in a study of the Bible itself. When one begins to go through these studies, he or she should have both the Old and New Testaments at hand.

The best way to use these studies is to look up each individual verse in the Bible, to read the verse with care, and then to read the statement that is made in the studies about that verse. The statements are not supposed to be complete explanations of any of the verses. Instead, they point out one specific thing that is taught in the verse, as that one specific thing bears on the teaching of that particular lesson. For example, the first Bible reference given (Ephesians 1:4) has many rich things in it that are not mentioned in the statement following it. But attention is called to just one of the things that Ephesians 1:4 teaches—that God, being a personal God, thinks. Thus, each verse should be looked up and considered in the light of the statement that immediately follows it—not merely as an isolated statement, but in the light of that whole lesson, and in the light of the flow of the unity of the biblical teaching as it is set forth in the complete twenty-five studies. The Bible is not just an unrelated group of verses. It is a unit. And it has content that can be studied as one studies other books.

Studied in this way, the Bible will be seen to have many things to say in answer to the questions that people are asking in our generation about the meaning and purpose of life. It tells us who Man is, Man's purpose, the source of Man's problems, and the solution to those problems. Of course, this study is just a beginning to help us begin studying the Bible. The Bible is a unit, and eventually we should read it all and see the relationship of each part to the whole. The unity of the Bible begins at the beginning, Genesis, and goes to the end, the book of Revelation.

Using verses as I have used them in these *Twenty-five Basic Bible Studies* has a danger that must be recognized and leaned against. That danger is choosing certain "proof texts" isolated from the context, and forcing all the rest of the Bible's teaching into our understanding of that one text. This is a danger. No one verse can give the whole Bible's richness. Each verse is to be taken in context if it is to be rightly understood. There are three contexts of each verse we study: (1) the immediate context; (2) the whole book in which the verse is located, and this includes the careful consideration of the purpose of that book; (3) the whole Bible and its teaching.

The whole Bible's teaching gives us a series of balances that no one verse can give. This takes a lifetime of careful study.

However, as I have used the verses I have tried to use them fairly—using my lifetime of study of the whole Bible as the background of the use of each verse as I have used it here.

Thus, these *Twenty-five Basic Bible Studies* are just that: basic teaching to open the door for a lifetime of studying the Bible. With the entire table of contents in mind as you study, it is hoped that these studies will provide a framework to understand the wonder of the flow of the whole Bible, from Genesis to Revelation. Then a lifetime of careful and prayerful study will show that these twenty-five studies are indeed only a beginning. I do think though that you will find that as I have used the verses I have taken into account the whole Bible's teaching.

As you do these studies it is not necessary to do a whole study at a time. If desired, one may spend a specific amount of time each day. When that time is reached, simply draw a line and start at that point the next day.

It would be my advice that each time you do these studies, you speak to God and ask Him to give you understanding through the use of the Bible and the study together. If someone pursues these studies who does not believe that God exists, I would suggest that you say aloud in the quietness of your room: "O God, if there is a God, I want to know whether You exist. And I ask You that I may be willing to bow before You if You do exist."

Francis A. Schaeffer

SECTION ONE

God

C H A P T E R

O N E

THE GOD
OF THE BIBLE

The God of the Bible is personal.

Ephesians 1:4

Notice here that God has a plan, that He thinks.

Genesis 1:1

God not only thinks, He acts.

John 3:16

God not only thinks and acts, God feels. Love is an emotion. Thus the God who exists is personal. He thinks, acts, and feels, three distinguishing marks of personality. He is not an impersonal force, nor an all-inclusive everything. He is personal. When He speaks to us, He says "I," and we can answer Him "You."

Deuteronomy 6:4

The Old Testament teaches there is only one God.

James 2:19

The New Testament also teaches there is only one God.

But the Bible also teaches that this one God exists in three distinct persons.

Genesis 1:26
"Let us make." Here it is shown that there is more than one person in the Godhead.

Genesis 11:7
Here again is an emphasis on there being more than one person in the Godhead. In this verse, as in 1:26, the persons of the Trinity are in communication with each other.

Isaiah 6:8
Again we see that there is more than one person in the Godhead.

Matthew 3:16, 17
Each of the three persons is shown clearly here. Also read Matthew 28:19; John 15:26; 1 Peter 1:2.

Matthew 9:2-7
Jesus Christ claims the power of forgiving sins as His natural right, thus showing that He claims to be God.

Matthew 18:20
Jesus said He was everywhere at once, another claim to deity.

Matthew 28:20
As Jesus is through all space, He is through all time.

John 5:22
Jesus Christ is to be Judge of all mankind. Only God could do this.

John 8:58
Jesus said He was living before the time of Abraham. Abraham lived in 2,000 B.C.

John 17:5, 24
Jesus said that He lived with the Father and that the Father loved Him before the world was made.

2 Corinthians 5:10
Here again we are told Christ will judge the world.

John 1:1-3
These verses say that the person called "the Word" is God and made all things. Verses 14 and 15 of this same chapter show that "the Word" is Jesus Christ.

John 20:28
Thomas affirms that Jesus is God.

Thus, the second person of the Trinity is not only distinct from the first person, but He is equally God.

Luke 12:10, 12

Let us now think about the third person of the Trinity. These two verses show that He is God and just as much a person as the first and second persons of the Godhead.

John 15:26

The Spirit is again said to do something only a person can do.

John 16:7-14

The Spirit, or Comforter, is distinct from the second person and does things only a person can do. The Spirit is "He," not "it."

Acts 8:29

Only a person can speak.

Acts 13:2; 15:28; 16:6, 7

The Holy Spirit is a person.

Ephesians 4:30

The above passages show that the Holy Spirit thinks and acts; this verse shows He also feels.

2 Peter 1:21

The Holy Spirit is the person of the Trinity who gave us the Bible.

It is central and important to our Christian faith to have clearly in mind the facts concerning the Trinity.

Genesis 1:26; John 17:24

Communication and love existed between the persons of the Trinity before the creation.

2 Corinthians 13:14

The work of each of the three persons is important to us. Jesus died to save us, the Father draws us to Himself and loves us, and the Holy Spirit deals with us.

Romans 8:11, 14, 26, 27

The Holy Spirit is a person, and He indwells and leads the Christian and prays for him when the Christian does not know what to pray for himself.

CREATION

In our last study, we saw that the Bible sets forth God as one God but in three persons. We are not worshiping the Christian God unless we worship this God who is one but three persons.

Likewise, a person is not worshiping the Christian God as he should unless he recognizes that God is sovereign.

When we speak of God's sovereignty, two thoughts are in mind—His work of creation and His work of providence. When we speak of providence, we mean His dealings in the world now.

The following Bible study deals with the Bible's teaching on creation.

Revelation 4:11

God created all things of His own free will. He did not have to create. Before creation the triune God stood complete, and there was love and communication between the persons of the Trinity. Revelation 4:11 reads: "You are worthy, our Lord and our God, to receive glory and honor and power, for You created all things, and by Your will they were created and have their being."

Colossians 1:16, 17
Before God created, He dwelt alone.

Psalm 33:9
God created out of nothing. He created by fiat: He spoke and it was.

Genesis 1:1
The word "create" used here means to create out of nothing. God created matter out of nothing. He did not just shape preexistent matter but brought it into being. He did not make only the world, but the heavens and the earth—everything there is. He created all things out of nothing. They now have objective existence; they are not an extension of Himself or His essence.

Genesis 1:31
After God had created all things, He pronounced it all "good." All things were good as they were originally made. They were not only good in man's judgment, but in God's absolute judgment.

If God made us, then we have a responsibility to obey Him.

SECTION

TWO

God's Dealing
with Man

C H A P T E R

T H R E E

———————

GOD AND MAN

With this study we begin considering what the Bible tells us of the relationship between God and man.

Genesis 2:7

In this verse we are told that God formed the body of man out of the dust of the ground. However, man is more than a body.

Genesis 1:26

Man was made in God's image. This is man's glory, and it is this that sets him off from other creatures. What does it mean that man is made in God's image? Well, among other things it certainly means this: man is moral. This means he can make moral choices. Also, man is rational. This means that he can think. It also means that man is creative; we find that men everywhere make works of art. It is also the reason why man loves.

Genesis 1:31

As God made man, man was good, both in body and soul.

Genesis 3:8a

Notice the first phrase in this verse. Man is here shown to be in perfect harmony with God, so that man and God could walk together in the cool of the day. Being in harmony with God, man was also in full harmony with his wife, with nature, and with himself. There was no place for divided personality or schizophrenia in man as he was originally made. He had power to love and obey God, but as a free agent he could also transgress.

Genesis 2:16, 17
Here stand two parties—God and man. In this verse God states the condition to be met in order for man to continue in fellowship with God. The condition is simple. Man must show his love for God by obeying Him. If man disobeys God, death would be the result. This is more than physical death. Spiritual death, or separation from God, came immediately. Physical death means that which we usually speak of as "death." Eternal death comes at the Judgment. As man was faced with the choice of obedience or disobedience, he had these gracious provisions from God:

(1) He was made in the image of God (Genesis 1:26).

(2) He had constant fellowship with God (Genesis 3:8a).

(3) He was surrounded by a perfect environment (Genesis 2:8).

(4) He had a truly free choice, with power to obey or power to transgress. He was not a deterministically conditioned being. He was not programmed (Genesis 2:16, 17).

(5) The test was most simple, with both the command and penalty clearly stated (Genesis 2:16, 17).

Genesis 3:1-20
Adam and Eve willfully chose to disobey God.

Genesis 3:7
By trying to cover themselves with the work of their own hands, they showed that guilt had come upon them.

Genesis 3:24
They lost communion with God and were put out of the Garden. Both the body and soul felt the effects of sin.

Genesis 3:17, 18
The external universe is now abnormal. It is not as God made it. It was changed because of man's sin. All that was under man's dominion was affected.

Romans 5:12, 17
Since Adam's fall, all men are sinners. Each time we look upon

the body of one who has died, it should remind us that man is a sinner.

Isaiah 53:6
Jeremiah 17:9
Romans 3:10-12, 23
Galatians 3:10

The following two passages point out to us that those who are now Christians were "children of wrath" before they accepted Christ as their Savior.

Ephesians 2:2, 3
Colossians 1:21

It would be well to close our consideration with the fact that each of us personally has sinned in God's sight (1 John 1:10).

In conclusion, God made man. Man's body and soul were good. Man had a true, unprogrammed choice by which he could show his love for God by obedience. Man had continued fellowship with God. He was in a perfect environment. He was given a simple test so that he could demonstrate his love and obedience. Adam and Eve sinned. Since then all people, including you and I, have personally sinned.

John 3:18, 36

Having sinned, we are under the judgment of God, under His condemnation, *now.*

GOD'S GRACE
(A)

Romans 6:23

Every one of us has earned only one thing at the hand of God, and that is judgment. As far as God's holiness and justice are concerned, He owes us nothing but judgment. He has made us, and we have sinned. But the last part of this verse tells us that in spite of this, because of His love, God has provided us with a way of approach to Him. It is not because God owes it to us; it is a gift based on His love. Adam and Eve were given a way of work that could please God. However, they sinned, and we also have all sinned, and thus this new approach that God gives us cannot be on the basis of our work, but on God's grace.

John 3:15, 16

Here we have the triune God standing with His arms open, telling us that even though we are sinners He has provided a way through which "whosoever will" may come.

Philippians 2:7, 8

How can the holy God say "whosoever" to sinners? God cannot just overlook our sin, because He is holy. If He did that, no moral

absolute would exist. We can come to God through grace, because
Christ worked for us. This finished work is His death upon the cross.

Romans 3:24-26
Because Christ died in substitution, God remains righteous, there
is a moral absolute, and yet we do not need to come under His
judgment.

John 3:15; 17:4
This is a gift to us, but only on the basis of Christ's perfect work.

1 Peter 1:18, 19
We are purchased with an infinite price.

John 6:29
Christ had to work for us, in His death. But because of His perfect
work, we now can approach God simply by faith, without works.

John 3:15, 16
God's promise is clear. If we accept Jesus as our Savior, then on
the basis of Christ's finished work (which we accept by faith
alone), we have God's promise of an eternal life. Faith is the
empty hand that accepts the gift.

John 3:18, 36
God's penalty is also clear. Because we are sinners, we are
already under the condemnation and judgment of God. If we
refuse God's gift, if we do not accept Christ's work for us, we
remain under the condemnation and judgment of God.

Hebrews 2:3
Adam was commanded to obey God, and he sinned. We have all
sinned. Therefore, we have earned spiritual, physical, and eternal
death. Now God in His love has given us another opportunity.
This is not of works, but of grace, in which we partake if we
accept His gift. If we accept Christ as our Savior and trust Him
only for our salvation, if we believe on Him and accept His death
for us, then we have eternal life. If we refuse God's gracious pro-
vision, we stay where we are, under the condemnation and judgment of God.

GOD'S GRACE
(B)

Genesis 3:15, 21

As soon as man sinned, God gave the promise of the coming Savior. He did this in words in verse 15 and by illustration in verse 21. After man sinned, he tried to cover himself with the works of his own hands (verse 7). God took this away and provided a covering of skins. To do this, an animal had to be slain. This was an immediate picture that the way man could come to God, now that he had sinned, was not by the humanistic works of his own righteousness, but by that which God would provide through the death of the coming Messiah.

Genesis 4:3-5

It would seem that God told Adam and Eve how He wanted them to worship in the future, through the presentation of a lamb as a picture of the coming Messiah. Abel did this, but Cain tried to come on the basis of his own works. Hebrews 11:4 tells us that Abel believed God; Cain did not.

Genesis 12:1-3

The promise that was given to Abraham, 2,000 years before Christ came, was twofold—national but also personal. The national promises were and are to the Jews. The spiritual promises were and are to all who would believe God and thus be in right relationship to the coming Messiah. This Messiah would be one of Abraham's descendants, humanly speaking.

Genesis 22:1-18
Here we have a clear picture in space-time history of the coming Messiah and His substitutionary work. The Old Testament saints had a much clearer concept of Christ's work than we usually attribute to them. Verse 14 ties the events of this chapter at 2,000 B.C. into the coming death of Christ 2,000 years later. This geographical location was later the geographical location of Jerusalem, where Jesus died. Compare verse 14 with 2 Chronicles 3:1.

Exodus 20:24, 25
Immediately after the Ten Commandments were given, God, in anticipation of man's inability to keep them, provided a way of approach to Him. This building of an altar without man's work on it looked forward to the promise of the Messiah, whose work would have none of man's work added to it. No man has ever kept the Ten Commandments perfectly.

Isaiah 53
Now, 700 years before Christ, we see again that the Jews were informed explicitly concerning the work of the coming Messiah. Incidentally, the whole sacrificial system of the Old Testament was a preview of the work of the coming Messiah. The Messiah would come and die for us.

Luke 2:25-32, 36-38
When Jesus was brought to the Temple as a baby, Simeon recognized Him for who He was: the Messiah prophesied in the Old Testament. There was a remnant in that day who had their personal faith fixed in the coming Messiah. Notice that Anna not only recognized Jesus as the Messiah, for whom she had been looking throughout her life, but she immediately went to tell others in Jerusalem who also had their personal faith fixed in the coming Messiah.

Romans 4:1-3
This states that Abraham, 2,000 years before Christ, was saved exactly as we are saved—through faith, without works.

Romans 4:6-8

David (1,000 years before Christ) was saved by faith, just as we are saved. The Ten Commandments had been given through Moses 500 years before David's time. Yet David is clearly said to have been saved not by works, but by faith. No man has ever been saved by his own humanistic works.

Romans 4:10, 11

After Abraham was saved by faith, he was later circumcised. Circumcision did not save him. It was merely an external sign of the fact that he had already been accepted by God through faith alone. No *religious* good works on our part can help us before the perfect God.

Romans 4:20, 22-25

Abraham was accepted by God because of faith, his believing what God had promised. The same is true of us.

Galatians 3:13, 14

When we receive Christ as our Savior by faith, we receive the same blessing of God Abraham received by faith.

Galatians 3:24

If all this is true, what good then is the law of God, the Ten Commandments, and the other eternal commandments given by God in the Old and New Testaments? The law is meant by God to show us that we are sinners, so that we see our need of accepting Christ as our Savior.

Hebrews 11:1-12:2

A long list is given of those who in the Old Testament times had faith in God. We who have these to look back upon are told to have the same faith in God, through the acceptance of Christ as our Savior.

Thus through all the ages, before Christ and after Christ alike, there is one way of salvation. All men have sinned. Salvation is available only through faith on the basis of the Messiah's finished work for us.

OLD TESTAMENT PROPHECIES OF THE COMING MESSIAH

After Christ was raised from the dead, He met a number of disciples on the road to Emmaus, but they did not recognize Him. We are told that before He made Himself known to them, He talked to them, and this is what the Bible says about it:

And beginning at Moses and all the prophets, he expounded unto them, in all the scriptures, the things concerning himself.
Luke 24:27

In other words, on the way to Emmaus He went back into the Old Testament and told them many things that the Old Testament had said concerning Him, which He had fulfilled in His life, death, and resurrection. The following are some of the Old Testament passages that foretold the coming of the Messiah. The word Messiah *in Hebrew is the same as the word* Christ *in Greek, and so one is merely the Old Testament word and the other the New.*

The following does not exhaust these Old Testament references. They are only a cross section.

Genesis 3:15

Man had just sinned. God made man perfect and gave him opportunity to obey God and show his love for Him. Instead of that, man disobeyed. God then gave a promise to mankind that a Messiah would come, One who would win the victory. This Messiah would come "born of a woman" (see Galatians 4:4).

Genesis 9:26

Time has passed. We are now in the days of Noah. Now the promise that in Genesis 3:15 was given to the whole human race is narrowed down to one portion of the human race—the Semitic peoples. The Semitic people today include such races as the Assyrians, Babylonians, Egyptians, Hebrews, Arabians, and a number of others.

Genesis 12:3

More time has passed again. Now, of all the Semitic people, the promise of the coming Messiah is given to one man, Abraham. The coming Savior would be born from his family—i.e., of the Jews.

Genesis 49:10

After Abraham there came Isaac, then Jacob, who had twelve sons. In this passage we are told from which of these twelve families the Messiah would come. He would be born of the tribe of Judah.

Exodus 12:46

We now enter another phase of the picture that is being drawn of the coming Messiah. This was written about 1,500 years before Christ. The passages given above occurred even before that time. Here Moses is saying that in regard to the passover lamb, which prefigured the coming of the Messiah, none of its bones would be broken. Notice how carefully John 19:36 points out that no bones of Christ were broken, even though He was crucified and even though this was not the case with the two thieves who were crucified with Him.

Deuteronomy 18:15

We are still about 1,500 years before Christ. Moses here gives a different line again concerning the Coming One. We are told here something of His work. When He comes, He will be an unusual and unique "prophet." A prophet, according to Scripture, is not basically one who tells the future, but rather one who speaks for God to men.

2 Samuel 7:16

The line is now narrowed down again. Of all the tribe of Judah, the Christ must come from a certain family. That family is the royal family of David. See Matthew 1:1 and 22:42.

Psalm 2:2

The picture of the coming Christ has grown more clear—what He must be, how He must act, what He must do if He is to be really the Messiah, the Savior of the world. In verse 7 we are told that this One is to be more than a man; God calls Him His Son. See Acts 13:33; Hebrews 1:5. Verse 12 urges each man to come into right personal relationship with this Messiah.

Psalm 16:8-11

Here we are told another thing about the Messiah. He will die, but His body will not remain in the grave. He will be raised from the dead. See Acts 2:25-31.

Psalm 22:1-18

This is a tremendous picture of the crucifixion of Christ. The Jews did not crucify; they stoned to death. The only nation that would crucify as a general practice would be the Romans. This passage in the book of Psalms was written about 1,000 years before Jesus lived and died, and long before the Romans came to prominence. Yet the picture given here of Jesus' death is a perfect picture of crucifixion. Notice too the many other details fulfilled at Christ's death.

Psalm 41:9

When this Messiah would come, He would be betrayed by one who had been close to Him. Jesus was so betrayed, of course, by Judas. See John 13:18; Acts 1:16.

Psalm 69:9

This is quoted concerning Jesus when He cleansed the Temple of those who had turned it into a place of commerce. See John 2:17.

Psalm 69:21

When Jesus was dying, this is exactly what happened to Him. See Matthew 27:34.

Psalm 110:1-4

Moses, 500 years before this psalm was written, said that the Messiah would be a prophet. This passage tells us he would also be a priest. A priest is very different from a prophet. A prophet speaks for God to men; a priest represents men before God. See Acts 2:32-35.

Isaiah 7:14

Here we have a stupendous sign. When the Messiah came, He would have a human mother but no human father. See Matthew 1:23.

Isaiah 9:6, 7

Notice the names given to the coming Messiah. Obviously He is to be more than a man; He is also to be God.

Isaiah 42:1-3, 6, 7

We have already seen that this Messiah would be born of a woman, without a human father, and would be God. But He would also be a servant, and this servant would open the way of blessing for Jews and Gentiles as well. See Matthew 12:17-21; Luke 2:32.

Isaiah 50:6

Here we are told something of the things that Jesus would suffer. The New Testament says this is exactly what happened to Him. They hit Him. They beat Him. They did everything not only to hurt, but to humiliate Him. See Matthew 26:67; 27:26.

Isaiah 52:13 to the end of Isaiah 53

The Coming One was to be a priest in a very special way. He was to be a priest by bearing our sins Himself. He was to be a suffering Messiah, to die for us.

Jeremiah 31:15

The New Testament says this was fulfilled literally when the little children were killed by King Herod at the time of Jesus' birth, in Herod's attempt to kill the coming Messiah who the wise men said had been born. See Matthew 2:17, 18.

Micah 5:2

Here we are told the exact city where the Messiah would have to be born: the town of Bethlehem. This verse also says that He has existed from the days of eternity. See Matthew 2:6.

Zechariah 9:9

Now we come to the third part of the work of Christ. Moses said He would be a *prophet*. Psalms and Isaiah designated Him as a *priest*. Zechariah clearly says He is to be a *king*. Jesus literally fulfilled this passage when He came in triumphal entry into Jerusalem just before His death. See Matthew 21:5.

Zechariah 11:11-13

We are told here exactly how much Judas would receive for betraying Christ. See Matthew 26:15.

Jesus fulfilled each of these literally. The possibility of any one man having done all these things, let alone being all that was designated, was impossible as a matter of coincidence. Jesus fulfilled them all because He is what the Bible says He would be. He is God, and also man born of a virgin, the One promised for thousands of years. When He came, all these things came to pass. These, then, are just a few of the things that Jesus must have talked about with the disciples on the road to Emmaus.

CHRIST THE MEDIATOR—
His Person

1 Timothy 2:5

Notice that this verse says there is only one mediator between God and man. That one mediator is the man Christ Jesus. There are not several possible mediators; Jesus Christ is the only one. He is the only possible intercessor between God the Father and man.

(1) First of all, let's review some of our observations in a previous study, "The God of the Bible." You will remember that in this we saw that the Bible teaches that Jesus Christ is God, equally God as is God the Father. We saw that the second person of the Trinity was God before He was born to Mary; He was God while He was on the earth; and He is God now. We also saw that the second person of the Trinity is distinct from the first person of the Trinity, the Father, and from the third person of the Trinity, the Holy Spirit.

(2) The Bible also teaches that Jesus Christ is truly man. In our day most heresies deny the true deity of Christ, but in the early church the common heresy was the denial of the true humanity of Christ. We should remember that from God's viewpoint, it is far more wonderful that the second person of the Trinity

became a man than that He is God. He had been God for eternity; He became a man when He was born.

Matthew 4:2
Christ became hungry.

Matthew 8:24
He slept.

Matthew 26:38
Jesus Christ had a soul as well as a body.

Luke 1:32
On His human side, Christ descended from a human family.

Luke 2:40, 52
He grew physically and mentally.

Luke 22:44
Christ suffered anguish.

Luke 23:46
He died.

Luke 24:39
After His resurrection, He still had a true body.

John 11:33, 35
Jesus wept.

John 19:28
Christ suffered thirst.

John 19:34
He had blood in His veins.

Romans 5:15
Adam was a man, and Christ was a man.

Galatians 4:4
This verse tells us that God the Father sent His Son, and that He, the Son, was born of a woman—as we all are born.

1 Timothy 3:16
This verse tells us that God revealed Himself in the flesh.

When men looked at Jesus Christ, they saw only one person, but He had two natures. He is truly God and truly man.

Hebrews 2:14, 18

God became man in order to become our mediator.

Hebrews 4:15

Our mediator knows how we feel, even in our temptations.

1 John 4:1, 2

The Bible says that it is most important to believe that Jesus had pre-existence and that at a point of history He came as a man. In this verse, we are told that it is upon this point that we are to test religious teachers, spirits, and systems. If they do not teach Jesus' pre-existence and that He became truly a man, they are not Christian.

(3) How did the unique Son of God become a man?

Isaiah 7:14

Seven hundred years before Jesus was born, it was prophesied that He would be born of a virgin. See Matthew 1:23. The Greek word used in Matthew can only mean "virgin" in its normal sense of the word.

Galatians 4:4

Notice that Paul says that Christ was born of a woman. In this important verse, dealing with the incarnation, no father is mentioned, and this would have been against Jewish usage if He had had a father.

Genesis 3:15

In this first promise of the coming Savior, the seed of the woman is mentioned. No father is mentioned.

Luke 1:27-38

It is interesting that Luke was a doctor, and that he gives the most detail about the virgin birth of Christ. Note verse 34.

Matthew 1:18-25

Joseph had the most to lose if Jesus was not virgin-born. But he was convinced that Mary had not been unfaithful, that the child to be born to Mary would have no human father, and that God alone was the child's father. The fact that Joseph was convinced after his original suspicion of Mary is strong testimony of the virgin birth.

Thus, concerning the person of Christ the mediator, He has always been God. Ever since He was born to Mary in the vir-

gin birth, the incarnation, He has been one person with two natures. He is truly God and truly man forever.

This is the one who is our mediator. There is no other.

CHRIST THE MEDIATOR—
His Work: Prophet

When we think of the work of Christ as mediator, we usually think of His death. This is especially true in our day because many people who have departed from the teaching of the Bible put all their emphasis on the moral facets of Christianity. Therefore, we in reaction are apt to speak only of the death of Christ. However, the Bible teaches us that there are three parts to Christ's work.

First, Christ is a prophet. A prophet is one who reveals the things of God to men. This is the giving of true knowledge, propositional knowledge.

Luke 13:33
Christ here says that He is a prophet.

Deuteronomy 18:15, 18
The Old Testament said the coming Messiah would be a prophet. Compare this passage with Acts 3:22, 23, which states that Christ fulfilled this.

John 1:18
However, Christ is not just *a* prophet. He is a *unique* prophet. He is the person of the Godhead who reveals the triune God to man.

John 1:1, 2

Here Christ is called "the Word" (see verses 14, 15). This signifies the fact that He is the one who reveals truth to men. Verses 14 and 15 make clear that "the Word" is Jesus Christ.

Colossians 2:9

While on the earth, Christ revealed the triune God to men. By considering Christ, we can learn about the character of God; and Christ taught men facts concerning the past, present, and future by His spoken words.

1 John 5:20

Christ came in the incarnation to give us true knowledge.

John 14:26; 16:12-14

Here Christ promises that after His death, resurrection, and ascension He would still continue to give knowledge to men through the Holy Spirit who was coming.

CHRIST THE MEDIATOR— His Work: Priest

Since man has fallen into sin, he needs more than knowledge. He also needs holiness and righteousness. Thus, Christ not only acts as a prophet, in giving us knowledge, but also acts as a priest. As priest, He removes the guilt of sin from us and provides for us true holiness and righteousness.

Psalm 110:4
This Old Testament prophecy predicted that when the Messiah came, He would do a priestly work.

Mark 10:45
Christ came to die. This was His great priestly work.

John 1:29
John called Christ "the Lamb of God," thus signifying that Christ would die to take away the guilt that is ours because of sin. By the term "Lamb of God," John also showed that the Old Testament sacrificial system was a type or illustration of the work Christ would do for us in a complete and final way by His death. That death was the act that the Old Testament sacrifices had foreshadowed.

1 Corinthians 5:7
Christ is here called our "Passover lamb," and He died for us. The

Passover lamb of Exodus 12 was a type or illustration of the work that Christ would do for those who believe on Him.

Ephesians 5:2
This verse says specifically that Christ gave Himself in His death as an offering and a sacrifice.

Hebrews 3:1
The book of Hebrews gives more detail on the priestly work of Christ than any other biblical writing. This verse says Christ is our High Priest.

Hebrews 4:14; 6:20
Christ was our High Priest not only when He was on earth, but is now and forever.

Hebrews 5:5, 6
As a priest, Christ fulfilled the prophecy of Psalm 110:4.

Hebrews 7:26, 27
Christ's high-priestly work is different in three ways from that of the Old Testament priests:
(1) He is perfectly sinless.
(2) He made a sacrifice that will never need to be repeated.
(3) The sacrifice He offered was Himself.

Hebrews 8:1
Since His ascension Christ, our High Priest, is at the right hand of God the Father.

Hebrews 9:11-15
Again the Scriptures emphasize that the sacrifice was Christ Himself, and that when the sacrifice was once made, it never needed to be repeated. Being God, Christ's sacrifice (His death) had infinite value.

Hebrews 9:25-28
Again it is emphasized that Christ's sacrifice was once for all. Just as men die only once, just as certainly there cannot be (and does not need to be) any repetition of Christ's sacrifice.

Hebrews 10:11-14
The sacrifice was once for all. Because of who Christ the High Priest is, a single offering (His once-for-all death for us) is enough.

Hebrews 10:19-22

Once we have accepted Christ as our Savior, we can have confidence in the presence of the holy God.

1 Peter 3:18

In the Greek the word used clearly means "once for all." So Peter is saying that Christ's sacrifice cannot, and need not, be repeated. From this and preceding verses we have considered, it is clear that Christ as our priest gave Himself as the sacrifice upon Calvary's cross at a point of space-time history, so that He might once for all bear the punishment that we deserve because of the guilt of our sin.

1 John 4:10

Christ's work is substitutionary, the expiation of our sins—it is an atoning sacrifice. In other words, He took the punishment rightly due to us because of our sin.

1 John 2:1

After we accept Christ as our Savior, we should strive not to sin. But if we sin, Christ is on the right hand of God the Father as our advocate. Christ's sacrifice on the cross was complete; but He now continues His high-priestly work by interceding for us in Heaven. Remember Hebrews 4:14; 6:20.

Hebrews 9:24

Christ is in Heaven, in the presence of the Father, for us.

Hebrews 7:25

Christ's sacrifice being perfect, He continues his priestly work and is able to save us completely and forever.

John 17:9

This is the high-priestly prayer of Christ that He prayed shortly before His death. In this verse we see that Christ does not intercede for everyone. He prays for those who, by God's grace, have accepted Him as their Savior.

John 17:20

Christ interceded at that time, and does so now in Heaven. He intercedes for all who have believed on Him on the basis of the testimony of those who were firsthand witnesses. This testimony is given in the New Testament in connection with the Old.

Romans 8:34

Once we have accepted Christ as our Savior, neither Satan nor man can successfully condemn us, because Christ died for us and now intercedes for us.

Christ's intercession in Heaven is based upon the substitutionary atonement that He wrought for us when He died upon the cross. His intercession for us can never fail, because in His death He merits all He asks on our behalf. Christ is our priest; we need no other.

CHAPTER

TEN

CHRIST THE MEDIATOR—
His Work: King

Genesis 49:10

Here we have the first promise that the coming Messiah will be a king.

2 Samuel 7:16 (with **Matthew 1:1; 22:42**)

Here the Lord tells David that the coming Messiah will come from among his descendants. Thus the Messiah will be of the kingly line.

Psalm 2:6

Again we see the Messiah as king.

Isaiah 9:6, 7

We usually use this as one of the Christmas verses. But notice that it says specifically that the Messiah will be of the line of David; He will be a king.

Micah 5:2

This verse reaffirms the same point, that the Messiah will be a ruler.

Luke 1:31-33

The angel makes the promise to Mary that the child who will be born to her will be a Savior (His name will be "Jesus"). He will be the Son of the Most High, and on His human side He will be of the family of David. He will be a king.

Matthew 2:2
When the wise men came, they were looking for the King of the Jews. Verse 6 connects this with Micah 5:2.

John 1:49
Nathanael realized that Christ was the Messiah, the King of the Jews.

Luke 19:37, 38
On Palm Sunday, the Sunday before Christ's crucifixion, for one short moment Jesus was proclaimed as king. Verse 40 shows that Christ accepted this.

John 18:37
Christ here acknowledges before Pilate that He is king.

John 19:2, 3, 12, 14, 15, 19, 21, 22
When the people were mocking Jesus, they did it in such a way that they made fun of His kingship. Verse 12 seems to indicate that if He had rejected this claim, the case against Him would have collapsed.

Acts 17:7
After His death and resurrection, Jesus' followers still taught that Jesus was king.

Christ is king in three ways:

(1) Christ is head over all things now.

Matthew 28:18
Right now all power is given to Christ in Heaven and on earth.

Ephesians 1:20-22
Today Christ, at the right hand of God the Father, is head over all things for the Church.

(2) The second coming of Christ.

Hebrews 2:8
There will come a time when Christ will rule in a way that He does not rule now. See also 1 Corinthians 15:24, 25.

Acts 1:6, 7
Just before Christ's ascension, He was asked when He would establish His kingdom upon the earth. He did not say He never would do so, but that the time had not yet come.

1 Timothy 6:14, 15

When Christ comes back again, He will then be King of kings and Lord of lords in a new way.

Matthew 25:31-34

When Christ returns, He will judge as king.

Revelation 17:14; 19:16

Again we see Christ when He returns as King of kings and Lord of lords. The Bible tells us that at that time every knee shall bow before Him (Philippians 2:10, 11). This does not mean that every knee will wish to bow before Him, but will bow of necessity, even if the individual sinful heart is still in rebellion against Him.

(3) Christ, the king of our lives.

Colossians 1:13

When we accept Christ as our Savior, we step from the power of darkness into the kingdom of Christ. Thus, we who have received Christ are in His kingdom now.

Ephesians 5:23, 24

Christ is now head of the Church, which is made up of all who have accepted Him as Savior. Once we have done this, we are to obey Him.

Luke 19:11-27

In this whole passage, Christ teaches us that after we have accepted Him as our Savior, we, as now His servants, are responsible for serving Him and will be held accountable for the way we do serve Him. If we serve Him well, He will then say to us, "Well done, my good servant." Verses 14 and 27 contrast the servants with the citizens, "the subjects." Since God is Creator, everyone is His rightful subject, but there are those who are still in rebellion against Him.

When we have taken Jesus as our Savior, He should be the king and Lord of our lives now.

The story is told that when Queen Victoria was a young girl, she was present at a concert where Handel's Messiah *was played. Everyone stood when the music rang out, "King of kings, Lord of lords." When Victoria also rose, others who were with her restrained her, saying she should not stand, because she was queen. Victoria answered, "I am Queen of England, but Christ is my King of kings and Lord of lords." After we have accepted Christ as our Savior, then He should in reality be our king, just as He is our prophet and priest.*

CHRIST'S HUMILIATION AND EXALTATION

When we consider Christ's work as a whole, we find that it presents two aspects: His humiliation and His exaltation.

(1) Christ's humiliation.

John 17:5

Here Christ speaks of the glory that He had had with God from before the creation of the world.

Philippians 2:6, 7

When Christ came into the world, He humbled Himself, so that the Creator of all the universe became the servant.

John 1:14

The Creator (verse 3) took upon Himself the form of a man. He "became flesh."

Luke 2:7

When Christ was born, He was not born in a great human family, but in a very poor one. When He was born, there was not even a home to shelter Him or a room in the public inn; He was born in a stable.

John 7:52

Christ did not even come from a respected portion of the country, but from Galilee, which was looked down upon by the Jews.

Mark 6:3
His family was not one of the great ones of the community. Joseph, the husband of Mary, was a carpenter, and Jesus followed his trade.

Galatians 4:4
The great Lawgiver placed Himself under the law.

Philippians 2:8
The one who Himself deserved obedience from all creation became obedient.

Galatians 3:13
The righteous Judge of all the universe placed Himself under the curse of the law. He identified Himself with sinful mankind.

Matthew 4:1-11; Hebrews 4:15
The Holy One allowed Himself to suffer every temptation that mankind can know. Consider what pain it must have been for Him to be daily buffeted by the sin that permeates the world in which we live.

John 1:11
The Jews, who were His ancient people, rejected Him.

John 7:3-5
His own half-brothers—i. e., the natural children born to Mary and Joseph after Jesus' birth—rejected Him until after His death and resurrection.

Matthew 27:46
As He hung upon the cross, having taken upon Himself the sin of those who would trust Him as Savior, God the Father turned from Him. Christ's physical sufferings were great, but they were not the greatest part of His suffering.

Luke 22:47, 48
Judas, one of His friends, betrayed Him with a kiss.

Matthew 26:56
All His disciples forsook Him in His hour of need.

Matthew 27:11-50
Consider the various forms of humiliation and agony heaped

upon Jesus in these hours. Remember that this is God who allowed Himself to be so treated.

2 Corinthians 5:21
The eternally Holy One died as sin for us.

1 Peter 3:18, 19
Like natural man, His spirit and body were unnaturally torn asunder when He died. His body rested in the grave. His soul descended into Hades.

(2) Christ's exaltation.

Acts 2:25-31
At this point comes a great change. Through Christ's humiliation, His steps have been downward all the way. Now comes the increasing glory. First, while His body lay in the grave, it did not see corruption.

Luke 24:36-43
The human body and the human soul of Christ were reunited. It was not just Christ's spirit that rose from the dead. It was the complete man, with body and spirit reunited.

John 20:25-28
Christ's resurrected body was the same body that the disciples had known before His death. Thomas's conquered skepticism is one proof of the physical resurrection of Christ—of the fact that the body that came out of the garden tomb was the one that had been placed in it.

Acts 1:3
Jesus, with His resurrection body, was seen from time to time over a forty-day period. This is spoken of here as convincing proof.

Acts 1:9-11
After Jesus had showed Himself upon the earth for many days after His resurrection, He was taken up into Heaven. He went from one place, earth, to another, Heaven. His baptism began His public ministry (Matthew 3:13-17). His ascension showed it to be terminated.

John 14:2, 3
In this place called Heaven, Christ is now preparing a place for us.

Acts 2:32, 33
The exaltation of the Lord Jesus Christ continues.

Ephesians 1:20-22
The One who was spat upon and humiliated before the eyes of sinful men is now head over all things.

Revelation 19:9-16
When Christ comes back again to the earth, Gentile and Jew alike will know that the One they humiliated and crucified is what He claimed to be: the Old Testament-prophesied Messiah, the only Savior of men, King of kings, Lord of lords, and indeed truly God.

Salvation

C H A P T E R

T W E L V E

SALVATION—HOW?

With this study we begin a completely new topic. We've already looked at "God" and "God's Dealing with Man." This third topic is "Salvation"—how it is received and what it includes.

How do we obtain salvation? The Bible's answer, as we have already partially seen in our study of God's grace, is that salvation is obtained by faith in Christ plus nothing.

John 3:15, 16, 18

We have used these verses a number of times, but they are worth looking at again to see how clearly Christ says that salvation is received by faith in Him plus nothing.

John 3:36

John the Baptist emphasizes that salvation is through faith plus nothing.

Romans 3:9-20

By the deeds of the law—that is, by good works—no man is or can be just in the sight of God.

Isaiah 64:6

Even our best works are not good enough in the sight of the holy

God. Even when the outward acts are good, who can completely untangle all the mixed and complex motives that move us?

Galatians 3:24

God never gave the law (the Ten Commandments, the Sermon on the Mount, or any other commands) as though salvation would come through the keeping of it. As far as salvation goes, each of God's laws shows us that we need Christ.

Romans 2:1-3

Men do not even keep their own made-up norms, by which they judge others.

Acts 16:30-33

Just as moral good works cannot save us, so also religious good works cannot save us. Baptism is a sign of salvation, not the basis for it.

Romans 4:9-11

It was the same in the Old Testament. Abraham put his faith in God. Circumcision came later. Religious good works cannot save.

Romans 9:6

Not all the Old Testament Jews were true spiritual Israel. Neither today will church membership in itself save. Salvation is indeed ours only on the basis of faith in Christ plus nothing.

Romans 9:30-33

Those Jews who were not true spiritual Israel were those who tried to come to God on the basis of their religious and moral "good works" instead of by faith.

Galatians 2:16

Salvation is never on the basis of any kind of good works.

Romans 3:21-26

Good works cannot save us, but faith in Christ will. The word "freely" in verse 24 means "*gratis*." There is no cost to us.

John 8:24

There is only one way of salvation. If we do not accept Christ as our Savior, we remain under the judgment of God.

John 14:6

There are not many ways of salvation. There is only one way to

come to God the Father. There is no way to come to God the
Father except through Christ.

Acts 4:12

It is faith in Christ or nothing.

*As you finish looking up these verses, I urge you to consider
Christ's invitation: "Whoever comes to me I will never drive
away" (John 6:37). The* basis *is the finished, substitutionary*
death of Christ. *The* instrument *by which we accept the free gift
is faith. Faith has a double significance: it is believing God's
promises, and it is the empty hand that accepts the gift without
trying to add humanistic religious or moral good works to it.*

JUSTIFICATION

Romans 1:16

As the word "salvation" is used here and throughout the New Testament, it has a much wider meaning than is usually given to it today. Today it is often limited to becoming a Christian. The scriptural use of the term includes all those things in the past, present, and future that will come to the man or woman who has accepted Christ as his or her Savior. In this lesson, we will consider the first of these things—that is, justification.

Romans 3:20

We cannot be justified on the basis of our good works.

James 2:10

In order to be justified before God on the basis of our good works, we would have to be perfect, without one sinful act or sinful thought from our birth to our death. The word "gospel" means "good news." Telling a person to be good is not good news. For example, if a person were in jail for some crime and someone rushed up to him and shouted, "Good news!" the person looking through the bars would expect word of possible liberation. If the friend's message were instead, "Be good," it would be foolish and

cruel. So it is if we would say, "Be good" to the man already
bound by sin and marked with its guilt.

Romans 4:1-9, 22-25
Justification is the declaration on God's part that we are just in
His sight because He has imputed to us the obedience of
Christ. This means that God charges our sins to Christ's
account. It is not an infused righteousness within us. He attrib-
utes to us the obedience of Christ. Christ's obedience has two
aspects: His death to take away our true moral guilt, and His
perfect keeping of the law of God on our behalf. It is as if a little child enters a store and buys more than he can pay for. Then
the parent arrives and says, "Charge that to my account." The
child's debt is erased. The parent pays. When we are justified,
God charges the punishment due to the guilt of our sin to the
account of Christ.

Romans 5:1
Once we are declared just by God, there is peace between God
and us.

Colossians 2:13, 14
It is not that God overlooks our sins. God cannot do this, for He
is holy. It is that our sins have actually been punished in the sufferings of Christ upon the cross.

Isaiah 38:17; 43:25; Micah 7:19
When we have been declared just by God, it is as though God has
dropped the guilt of our sins into the deepest sea. The justification is not merely a pardon, but, as has been said, once we have
been justified, it is "just as though we have never sinned."

Isaiah 53:4, 5
The ground for our justification is the perfect work of Christ on
Calvary.

Romans 5:8, 9
This is the wonder of the love of God—that while we were sinners, Christ died for us. Because Christ has died for us, God can
be just and yet declare our sins forgiven (Romans 3:26).

Acts 13:38, 39
The instrument by which we lay hold of this great gift of God is
faith in Jesus Christ.

Romans 3:28
Justification is by faith plus nothing.

Galatians 2:16
There is only one way to be justified before the holy God, and that is by faith in Christ.

What is faith in Christ? A missionary when seeking a native word for faith could not find it. Finally he sat in a chair and raised his feet from the ground, putting his full weight on the chair and bearing none of his weight himself. He then asked what word described his act and used that word for faith. This is an accurate picture.

Faith in Christ is resting totally on Him and His finished work.

THE NEW RELATIONSHIP:
Adoption

When we accept Christ as our Savior, we are immediately justified. Another aspect of the salvation that is immediately ours is a new relationship—adoption by God the Father.

John 1:12

When we accept Christ as our Savior, we become the children of God. This indicates that we are not God's children until we do accept Christ. Before we accept Christ as our Savior, we are separated from God by our moral guilt. God made us all, but we are the children of God only as we come through Jesus Christ.

2 Corinthians 6:18

In most Bible verses men and women together are spoken of as "the sons of God." But here we have a very significant passage where God speaks of the women who come to him through Christ as His "daughters."

John 20:17

Christ is very careful to make a clear distinction between His unique and eternal Sonship and our becoming the children of God.

Galatians 4:4, 5

Christ is the eternal Son of God. He is unique. He is the only begotten Son. But when we take Christ as our Savior, we receive the adoption of sons. These verses say that on the basis of Christ's finished work, we receive the full rights of sons.

Ephesians 1:3-5

Once we have taken Christ as our Savior and so are God the Father's children, we may come into His presence with all boldness. As the child of a king may come into the king's presence as his child, so we may come into the presence of Almighty God, the Creator. We may rightfully say to Him, "Thou art our Father," and He says to us, "You are My children."

1 John 3:1

This is the consummation of God's love, that when we accept Christ as our Savior we are the sons of God.

Matthew 6:32

When I am a child of God, He is concerned about my material needs.

Romans 8:15

When God is our Father, we may call Him "Abba"—i.e., "Daddy" or "Papa."

Romans 8:17

When God is our Father, we are joint-heirs with Christ. Think what this means. The riches of Heaven are ours not only after death but in this life as well.

Galatians 4:6, 7

As soon as God becomes our Father, these blessings are ours, including the indwelling of the Holy Spirit. As sons of God, these blessings are ours in the present life.

Hebrews 12:5-11

Once God has become our Father, many blessings are ours, and among them is this: as a human father who deeply loves his child chastens his child when he is naughty, so God our Father brings things into our lives to keep us close to Himself. After we have taken Christ as our Savior, and God is our Father, our sins have been all punished on Calvary. But the Father at times allows hard things to come into our lives when we wander away from Him, so that our lives may experience "the peaceable fruit of righteousness," which is not only righteousness but peace.

THE NEW RELATIONSHIP:
Identified and United
with God the Son

After we have put our faith in Christ, we enter a second new relationship—we are identified and united with Christ.

Romans 8:1
After we have accepted Christ as Savior, we are in Christ.

1 Corinthians 6:17
We are joined to, united with, Christ.

Galatians 2:20
Christ lives in me.

Ephesians 1:3
We are in Christ.

Ephesians 1:6, 7; 2:1-6, 13
These verses all restate this glorious truth—we are in Christ. See also Colossians 2:10.

Christ is the Bridegroom; *we are the* bride.

Matthew 22:2-14; 25:10
Our union with Christ is like a marriage. Christ is the Bridegroom.

Romans 7:4
When we accept Christ as Savior, we are married to Christ. As

natural marriage brings forth children, so our union with Christ should produce fruit for God.

2 Corinthians 11:2
A bride who loves her husband has her mind only on him and is faithful to him. So we should have our minds fixed on Christ and be faithful to Him.

Ephesians 5:31, 32
Marriage is a picture of the believer's union with Christ.

Revelation 19:7-9
At the second coming of Christ, there will be a great event known as "the marriage supper of the Lamb [Christ]."

Revelation 22:17
The bride, those who have taken Christ as Savior, should be busy inviting others to partake in this high privilege and honor. As a bride talks very naturally about her beloved, so our conversation should be much about Christ.

Christ is the vine; *we are the* branches.

John 15:1-5
The life of the vine flows into the branches to bring forth fruit. In the same way, those who have accepted Christ as Savior have a vital union with Christ. If we "abide" in him moment by moment, His life flows into us to bring forth spiritual fruit.

Christ is the Head; *the Church (those who have received Christ as Savior) is the* body.

Romans 12:5
As the body has many parts, yet is one body, so we who have accepted Christ as Savior are many, and yet we are one body, the Church, the body of Christ.

1 Corinthians 12:11-27
As the body's health depends on the condition of all its parts, so it is important for all the Christians to be in good spiritual condition. As the body is subject to the direction of the head, so we should constantly do the bidding of Christ.

Ephesians 1:22, 23; 4:15, 16; 5:30; Colossians 1:18
The Church (all who have accepted Christ as Savior) is Christ's body.

Christ is the foundation; *we are the* spiritual house *built on it.*

1 Peter 2:2-6
We are living stones.

The only begotten Son of God is called our brother as we become the adopted children of God.

Hebrews 2:16-18
As the natural son of a household is the brother of the adopted child, so Christ is our wonderful Elder Brother when we take Him as our Savior. As our Elder Brother, He understands us in all the portions of our lives.

In our studies of Christ as mediator we have seen that when we take Christ as our Savior, God the Son is our prophet, priest, and king. Christ is our prophet, and in fellowship with Him the believer is a prophet.

John 16:13; 1 John 2:27
Through Christ we have true knowledge, knowledge that we should give to a dying world that is in confusion, intellectually lost in unrelatedness. God has given us the Bible to give us true knowledge, and it is our calling to give this true knowledge to others.

Christ is our priest, and in fellowship with Him every believer is a priest.

1 Peter 2:5, 9; Revelation 1:6; 5:10; 20:6
Every believer has the privilege of coming immediately into the presence of God in prayer. We should diligently avail ourselves of this privilege, including prayer for the non-Christians around us. We should seek to lead those who do not know Christ as Savior to Him, the great High Priest.

Romans 12:1, 2
Every believer has the privilege of offering himself to God as a living sacrifice.

Christ is our king, and with Him the believer is a king.

1 Peter 2:9; Revelation 1:6; 3:21; 5:10; 20:6
We are a *royal* priesthood. We are to praise God now, and we shall reign with Christ on the earth when Christ comes back again.

It is by being united with Christ that we can bring forth fruit in all the phases of our lives.

John 15:5
Abiding in Christ is the secret of fruit-bearing.

2 Corinthians 12:9
It is not our strength, but the strength of Christ in the midst of our weakness.

Ephesians 2:10
After becoming united with Christ, we should bring forth good works.

Philippians 1:11
The fruit we should bring forth after we are Christians must be by Christ working in and through us.

Colossians 2:10
We have all we need in Christ, for this life as well as for eternity.

CHAPTER

SIXTEEN

THE NEW RELATIONSHIP:
God the Holy Spirit
Indwells the Christian

*When we accept Christ as Savior, we have a third new rela-
tionship—God the Holy Spirit dwells within us.*

Joel 2:28, 29
The Old Testament prophesied this.

John 14:16, 17; 7:38, 39; 16:7; Acts 1:5
Christ promised this.

Matthew 3:11
John the Baptist so spoke concerning Christ.

Acts 2:1-18
The promise and prophecy were fulfilled after Christ had died,
had risen, and had ascended into Heaven.

Romans 8:9
There is no such thing as a person who has accepted Christ as
Savior who is not at once indwelt by the Holy Spirit.

1 Corinthians 3:16
The Holy Spirit dwells in all who have received Christ.

1 Corinthians 6:19
The body of the believer is the temple of the Holy Spirit. The

Temple in Jerusalem was destroyed a few years after this was written. Believers' bodies are now God's temple.

2 Timothy 1:14
The Holy Spirit lives in the Christian.

Here are some examples of the Holy Spirit's activity:

John 16:8
The Spirit reproves the world of sin. Because the Christian is indwelt by the Holy Spirit, his life should reprove the world of sin.

John 3:5, 6
Regeneration is the Spirit's work.

John 15:26; 16:14; Acts 5:32
He bears witness to Christ, not to Himself.

1 Corinthians 12:4, 13; Ephesians 2:22
He builds the Church (those who are real Christians) into a well-balanced whole.

2 Corinthians 13:14
The indwelling Spirit deals with the Christian. He communicates to the believer the benefits of redemption.

John 14:16-18; Romans 8:9-11
When the Holy Spirit dwells in us, Christ dwells in us.

John 14:23
When the Holy Spirit dwells in us, both the Father and the Son come to us, make their home with us. The indwelling Holy Spirit is the agent of the whole Trinity as He indwells us.

John 14:26; 15:26; 16:7; Acts 9:31
The indwelling Holy Spirit is the Christian's counselor. The Greek word translated "counselor" is a hard word to translate. It can also be comforter, advocate, protector, supporter. It means "one called to one's side to help."

John 14:26; 16:13; 1 Corinthians 2:12, 13; Hebrews 10:15, 16; 1 John 2:20, 27
The indwelling Spirit is our teacher, especially in opening our minds to understand the Bible.

Acts 1:8
He is the Christian's source of power.

Luke 12:11, 12
He gives the believer the right words in time of persecution.

Romans 5:5; 14:17; 15:13; 1 Thessalonians 1:6; Galatians 5:22, 23
The indwelling Spirit gives the Christian graces of love, joy, peace, hope, longsuffering, etc. As all Christians are indwelt by the Spirit, the fruit of the Spirit is to have meaning for all Christians.

The great distinction of a true Christian is the indwelling of the Holy Spirit. How careful should he be, lest anything in his thoughts or feelings would be offensive to this divine guest!
—*Dr. Charles Hodge*

This new relationship with the triune God is, then, the second of the blessings of salvation, justification being the first. This new relationship, as we have seen, is threefold:

(1) God the Father is the Christian's Father.

(2) The only begotten Son of God is our Savior and Lord, our prophet, priest, and king. We are identified and united with Him.

(3) The Holy Spirit lives in us and deals with us. He communicates to us the manifold benefits of redemption.

THE NEW RELATIONSHIP:
The Brotherhood of Believers

We have seen that when we take Christ as Savior we are immediately justified, and we immediately have a new relationship with God the Father, God the Son, and God the Holy Spirit.

When we come into this new relationship with the triune God, all those who have ever trusted Christ as their Savior are our brothers and sisters. This has been usually spoken of as "the communion of saints."

Matthew 23:8

Not all men are brothers, according to the biblical use of that word. We are all created by God. As all are descendants of Adam and Eve, all men are "my kind" and are to be carefully treated as neighbors (Luke 10:27-37). But in the terms of the Bible, we are brothers to those who have Christ as their Savior and therefore have God as their father.

Galatians 6:10

We are to do good to *all* men, but there is a clear line between the "family of believers" and others.

Ephesians 2:19

Before we took Christ as our Savior, we were strangers and foreigners. But when we became Christians, we were made fellow-citizens and members of God's household with all others who had done the same.

1 Thessalonians 5:14, 15
Again we are told to do good to all people, but again it is made clear that there is a distinction between those who are the "family of believers" and others.

1 Peter 2:17
We have a special relationship to those who are brothers in Christ.

1 John 1:3
A person cannot have true spiritual fellowship with Christians until he has heard the facts of the gospel and has acted upon those facts by accepting Christ as his Savior.

Revelation 19:10
The brethren are defined as those who hold to the testimony of Jesus.

John 13:30, 34, 35
Judas, who did not believe on Christ, had left the table before this command for special love among Christians was given.

John 21:23
It is clear that "brethren" as used here speaks of believers.

Acts 9:17
Saul was considered a "brother" only after he had taken Christ as his Savior.

Acts 21:17
Only the fellow-believers were "the brothers."

1 Corinthians 7:12
In this passage the man is a believer and therefore a brother. The wife is not a believer and therefore is not included in this term.

There are three practical aspects of the brotherhood of believers. The first practical aspect is that brothers in Christ should be a spiritual help to each other.

Romans 12:10
Christians should love one another and should desire the advancement of their brothers above their own advancement.

1 Corinthians 12:26, 27
Christians should sorrow when other Christians suffer, and should rejoice when other Christians have joy.

Romans 15:30; 2 Corinthians 1:11
Christian brothers are to pray for each other.

Ephesians 4:15, 16
When individual Christians become what they should be, the Church becomes what it should be. Each Christian has something to contribute to this.

Ephesians 5:21—6:9
The brotherhood of believers should be the predominant factor between Christians in all the relationships of life. This is true of husbands and wives, children and parents, servants and masters, employees and employers. In all such relationships we are also brothers and sisters. See Song of Solomon 4:9, 10, 12—there is a double relationship of sister and bride.

Ephesians 6:18
Christians should pray for each other and for all Christians. The brotherhood of believers cuts across the lines of nationality, race, language, culture, social position, and geographical location.

1 Thessalonians 5:11
The two great spiritual helps that brothers in Christ should be to each other are those of encouraging one another and edifying one another. The latter means helping other Christians to be what they should be in doctrine and life.

The second practical aspect is that brothers in Christ should be a material help *to each other.*

Acts 11:29
From the earliest days of the Church, Christians gave of their material goods to help those brothers in Christ who had less materially, even those at great geographical distance.

2 Corinthians 8:4
This is one of many examples given in the New Testament of

Christians giving money to help other Christians in material need.

Romans 12:13; Titus 1:8; Philemon 5, 7, 22
One form of practical help is by giving hospitality.

1 John 3:17, 18
There is no use talking about Christian love if we do not help our brothers in Christ when they have material needs.

Acts 5:4
The Christians helped each other materially, but they did it voluntarily. Each man kept the right of personal property and possession.

The third aspect is that brothers in Christ should enjoy the fellowship and companionship *of each other.*

Acts 2:42, 46
From the earliest days of the Church, the Christians had daily fellowship with each other.

Ephesians 4:1-3; Colossians 2:1, 2
True Christians should try to have fellowship together in love and peace.

Hebrews 10:25
It is the direct command of our Lord that after we have become Christians, we should meet together for worship with other Christians. This was not just to be a passing thing in the early days of the Church, but should continue even until Christ comes back again. This verse says we should be especially careful to keep this command as we come toward the time of the second coming of Christ. If we have accepted Christ as our Savior, we have the responsibility to search out a Bible-believing group of God's people, where there is right doctrine and real community in love, and meet with them. We should not join ourselves to just any group that calls itself Christian, but one where the teaching is truly biblical, where discipline is maintained concerning life and doctrine, and where there is true community. If there is no such group geographically available (and there are such places), then prayerfully before the Lord we should find even a small number to meet for worship, prayer, study, and encouraging one another and to have community.

We have seen that the brotherhood of believers crosses all the lines of space. It also crosses all the lines of time.

Hebrews 12:22, 23

This brotherhood includes not just Christians on the earth today, but Christians who are in Heaven.

CHAPTER

EIGHTEEN

NEVER LOST AGAIN

We have seen that salvation immediately includes justification and new relationship. Now we come to a third consideration: once we accept Christ as Savior, we will never be lost again.

Romans 8:31-34
We will never be lost again, because of the perfection of Christ's priestly work for us. The ground of our salvation is not our good works in the past, present, or future, but the perfect work of Christ. Christ's perfect priestly work includes two things: His perfect death and His perfect intercession for us now.

Hebrews 7:25
This one passage reminds us of everything we studied under Christ's work as priest, including His present intercession for us. You will remember that this verse teaches that the Lord saves us both completely and forever. The Christian could be lost again only if Christ failed as a priest.

Romans 8:28-30; Ephesians 1:3-7
After becoming Christians by accepting Christ, we learn that God the Father has chosen us. The Christian could be lost again only if the first person of the Trinity, the Father, failed.

Ephesians 1:13, 14

In days gone by when a man bought some land, he was given a handful of earth (an earnest or seal) to signify that all the land was his. The fact that the Holy Spirit now lives in us is a deposit guaranteeing that one day we will have all the benefits of salvation. We will not be lost again.

Ephesians 4:30

In past centuries a king would seal a document with wax and then mark the wax with his ring. No man then dared to break this seal except under the authority of the king. This passage says that God Himself has sealed us with the indwelling Holy Spirit unto the day of redemption—that is, until the day in which Christ will return and we will receive all the benefits of redemption. A rebel might break a human king's seal, but nothing that God has created can break the seal of God.

Romans 8:26

When we do not know how to pray for ourselves as we should, the indwelling Spirit prays for us. The Christian could be lost again only if the Holy Spirit failed.

John 10:27-29

Christ says that when we accept Him as our Savior, we have eternal life. Eternal life could be no shorter than eternity. Christ says we shall never perish; "never" can only mean "never." Christ says that nothing can pluck us out of His hand or the Father's hand. It's not that we hold fast to God; He holds fast to us.

Romans 8:35-39

Here God says specifically that no created thing can separate us from Himself after we have come to Him through Jesus Christ.

Philippians 1:6

"The day of Jesus Christ" is Christ's second coming, when we will receive the full benefits of salvation.

1 John 4:13; 5:13

Notice the use of the word "know." God wants us to have the assurance that we are His and will be forever.

2 Timothy 4:7, 8

Paul had this assurance.

Romans 8:15, 16

The assurance that we are God's children and that we will be His forever is one of the good things God means us to have after we have accepted Christ as Savior. Not all who are true Christians have this assurance; but if they do not, they have not taken advantage of one of the riches in Christ Jesus that it is their privilege to have now.

[handwritten margin note: Report of the Spirit]

John 3:36

"Whoever puts his faith in the Son has eternal life." If you know that you have believed in Christ for your salvation and are not trusting in your own moral or religious works, then you have the express promise of God that you do have everlasting life, *now and forever.*

C H A P T E R

N I N E T E E N

SANCTIFICATION
(A)

We have seen that once we accept Christ as Savior, we are jus-tified. We enter into a new relationship with each of the three persons of the Trinity. We will never be lost again. In this study we begin to consider another part of our salvation—sanctifi-cation. While justification deals with the past (once I have become a Christian), sanctification deals with the present. It has to do with the power of sin in the Christian's life. Justification is the same for all Christians, but obviously sanc-tification has proceeded further in some Christians than in others. For a book-length study of the subject of sanctification, see my book True Spirituality.

Romans 8:29, 30
Salvation is not a blank from the time we are justified until we reach Heaven. Rather, it is a flowing stream involving the past (when we became Christians), the present, and into the future. If we have truly taken Christ as our Savior, this has many implica-tions for our present lives, including the fact that our lives should show that we are Christ's.

Colossians 3:1-3
Once we have accepted Christ as personal Savior, it should make a difference in the lives we live.

John 15:1-5
If a man is truly a Christian, there should be some spiritual fruit in his life.

1 Thessalonians 5:23; Hebrews 13:20, 21
God the Father is active in our sanctification.

Ephesians 5:25, 26; Titus 2:11-14
So is God the Son.

1 Corinthians 6:11; 2 Corinthians 3:18; 2 Thessalonians 2:13
God the Holy Spirit is active in our sanctification.

Romans 12:1-19; 2 Corinthians 7:1; Colossians 3:1–4:6
These are just a few of the commands given in the Bible as to how we should walk in this life. As Christians, God's law is our rule of life. In such passages as these, God tells us what conforms to His character and what pleases Him. Being Christians should make a difference in every aspect of our lives.

1 Corinthians 6:20
We were saved by faith, not by good works. But after we are saved, we should show forth our gratitude in our lives by good works.

Matthew 22:37, 38; Revelation 2:1-5
The only proper basic motive for desiring to get over our sins and to grow spiritually is our love for God. Fear of getting caught, etc. will not do. We are to live a Christian life because we love the Lord and wish to glorify Him.

John 15:8
When a believer sins, he is not glorifying the Heavenly Father as he should.

Philippians 1:20
When a believer sins, he is not showing forth the glory of Christ in this present life, as a reborn person should.

Romans 8:9; Galatians 5:16-25; Ephesians 5:18; 4:30;
1 Thessalonians 5:19
When a person accepts Christ as Savior, he is indwelt by the Holy Spirit immediately and from then on. But when a believer sins, he is walking after the flesh and not after the Spirit. He is grieving (making sad) the Holy Spirit who indwells him and is putting out the Spirit's fire.

1 John 1:3, 7; 2:1

When a Christian sins, he does not lose his salvation. The blood of Christ is enough to cover the sin; and Christ, at the right hand of the Father, intercedes for the Christian. But a Christian does break his fellowship with God when he sins. If a child is disobedient, he does not cease being a child of his parent. But the joy of the child-parent relationship is gone. As long as our fellowship with our Heavenly Father is broken because of sin, we cannot expect spiritual power or joy.

Hebrews 12:5-11

When a believer sins, God chastens him in this life, even as a loving human parent chastens his child. God does not do this to punish us, for our sins were punished once for all on Calvary, but to bring forth the peaceable fruit of righteousness in our lives. However, it is most important to remember that not all the troubles of life are the result of personal sin. For example, consider the trials of Job.

2 Corinthians 5:9, 10; 1 Corinthians 3:11-15; Luke 19:11-27

In the future life, the Christian will receive rewards, which will depend on the life now lived after he has become a Christian. In Luke notice the distinction between the Christians (servants), who receive rewards, and the non-Christians (subjects and enemies), who are put aside.

1 Corinthians 11:31, 32

When a Christian sins, his fellowship with God can be restored. The first thing necessary is to acknowledge that the thing we have done is sin. As surely as God the Father is our Father, if we do not do this He will chasten us—not to punish us, but to bring us back to Himself.

1 John 1:9

After self-judgment, acknowledging his sin to be sin, the believer must confess his sin to God—not to a priest or any other man, but directly to God. He is our Father, and in prayer we can come into His presence at any time. We must bring the specific sin under the finished work of Christ. Then our fellowship with God is restored. After this confession, the matter is finished, unless I have injured other people by my sin. Then, of course, if am repentant, I will desire to make restitution.

1 John 1:8
The process of sanctification goes on until death. By God's grace, the Christian always has new ground to win for Christ.

SANCTIFICATION
(B)

Matthew 5:48

While we will always have new ground to gain for Christ in our lives, our standard for every moment must be no lower than God's command—that is, perfection.

Ephesians 4:12, 13; 2 Peter 3:18

While it is a comforting truth that when a Christian sins he can confess his sins and have his fellowship with God restored, yet our Christian lives should be something more than always sinning and confessing the same old sins.

Romans 6:1-19

If we have partaken of the benefit of Christ's death for justification, we should also be partakers of the power of His life, so that we should no longer serve sin—sin should not reign in us and through us. As we yield to Christ at this one moment, He will bring forth His fruit through us.

2 Corinthians 13:14

As seen in our studies of the "new relationship" we have with God, we have a personal relationship with each of the three members of the Trinity. Our relationship is never mechanical and not

primarily legal. It is personal and vital. God the Father is my
Father; I am united and identified with God the Son; God the
Holy Spirit dwells within me. The Bible tells us that this threefold relationship is a present fact, just as it tells us that justification and Heaven are facts.

*We have seen that once we are saved, we always are saved, but
that some Christians do not have this confidence, simply because
they have never realized what the Bible teaches concerning
assurance or, knowing the facts, they have not rested on them.*

*It is also possible to be a Christian and yet not take advantage
of what our vital relationship with the three persons of the
Trinity should mean in living a Christian life. We must first intellectually realize the fact of our vital relationship with the triune
God and then in faith begin to act upon that realization. At this
point I would urge you to glance again over the three studies on
our "new relationship" with the Father, Son, and Holy Spirit.*

Ephesians 3:14-19; 2 Corinthians 12:9
It is not my weakness but the triune God's strength that counts.

1 John 5:3-5
The victory that overcomes the world is our faith. (It is not that the
ground is our faith; in sanctification, as in justification, the only
ground is the perfect, finished work of Christ.) The Bible tells us
both the fact of justification and the fact of our present vital relationship with the Trinity. But mere intellectual acceptance is not
enough in either case. Knowing the facts, we must rest upon them
in faith. Justification is an *act*; I throw myself on Christ as Savior
once, and God declares me justified forever. Sanctification is a
process that begins when I take Christ as my Savior and continues
until I die. Thus, for my daily walk as a Christian, I must by God's
grace rest in faith upon my present vital relationship with the three
persons of the Trinity for every moment of my life. In both justification and sanctification I must see that I cannot keep God's law in
my own strength. Therefore, for my justification I must have rested
in faith in Christ as my Savior; in sanctification moment by moment
I must throw myself upon the fact of my present vital relationship
with Father, Son, and Holy Spirit. The Bible tells me that this vital
relationship is a fact. Through faith I lay hold of this fact for this one
moment, and all of life is only a succession of moments—one

moment at a time. Thus, by God's grace, "his commands are not burdensome." And by God's grace I may have spiritual power and the Lord will be my song.

SANCTIFICATION (C)

1 Peter 2:2; John 17:17; Acts 17:11; Acts 20:32;
Ephesians 5:26; 2 Timothy 2:15

There are four practices that help us greatly to grow spiritually. The first is the study of the Bible, which is the Word of God.

Philippians 4:6; 1 Thessalonians 5:17

The second is prayer. We should cultivate the habit of two types of prayer:

(1) Special times of prayer: for example, morning and evening, grace at meals, and from time to time special days of prayer.

(2) Praying constantly as we go about our daily tasks.

Acts 1:8

The third is witnessing for Christ. This command is to all Christians. You can do your part; you can be a "teller" no matter where the Lord places you in life.

Hebrews 10:24, 25; Acts 2:46, 47

The fourth is regular attendance at a Bible-believing church. As we saw under "The Brotherhood of Believers," this does not mean just any church or group, but one that is true to the Word

of God—one that has an orthodoxy of doctrine and an orthodoxy of love and community. To repeat what was said under
"The Brotherhood of Believers": If there is no such group geographically available (and there are such places), prayerfully
before the Lord we should find even a small number to meet for
worship, study, prayer, and encouraging one another and to have
community.

*In connection with our attendance at a Bible-believing church,
we also have the privilege of partaking in the Lord's Supper.*

*It is wonderful to know that we are justified and that we will be
in Heaven. But our present desire should be to glorify the triune God because we love the Father, because we love the Son,
because we love the Holy Spirit.*

GLORIFICATION AT DEATH

As we have previously seen, our salvation includes things past, present, and future. If we have accepted Christ as Savior, justification (God's declaration that our guilt is covered) is past. Sanctification deals with the present. Glorification is that which comes to a Christian at death and afterwards.

2 Thessalonians 1:4-10
The Bible speaks here of that which all of us can observe in the world about us. It is obvious that the accounts of life are not balanced in this life. Christians are often persecuted, while wicked men seem to prosper. This passage of Scripture teaches that the very fact that these inequalities take place in this life proves that in the future there will be a judgment by God, who is perfectly just. The books will be balanced.

John 3:36
When we accept Christ as our Savior, we are promised not a salvation that terminates with this life, but an everlasting, an eternal, salvation.

Ecclesiastes 12:7
Notice the clear distinction made here between the body and the soul at death. Physical death is the separation of soul and body.

Luke 23:39-43

When the Christian dies, the body goes into the grave, but the soul is immediately with Christ.

Acts 7:54-59

At the Christian's death the soul is immediately in Christ's presence.

2 Corinthians 5:6, 8

For the Christian, death is not something to fear. It brings us entrance into that which is better than we now possess. This does not change the fact that death is abnormal, caused by the Fall.

Luke 9:28-36

Moses died and was buried about 1,500 years before this event took place. But the disciples recognized him, even though they had never seen him and even though, as far as we know, his body was still in the grave. When we die, we can expect to know our loved ones and other Christians, even though their bodies are still in their graves.

C H A P T E R

T W E N T Y - T H R E E

GLORIFICATION AT THE RESURRECTION

Genesis 2:7
God made our bodies as well as our souls.

Genesis 3:1-20
Man's fall into sin involved the complete man, both body and soul. Because man sinned, three deaths came upon him. Spiritual death (separation from God) came immediately. Physical death is what we usually speak of as "death." Eternal death will come at the final judgment. When we take Christ as our Savior, the first and third of the above three deaths are finished for us. Our fellowship with God is restored, and our sins have been punished once for all on Calvary. The second death, the separation of soul and body at death, has yet to be dealt with.

Romans 8:23
We have the "first fruits of the Spirit," but there is still the last step to be realized—"the redemption of our bodies."

1 Corinthians 15:12-26
As Christ rose physically from the dead, so the bodies of Christians will also be raised physically. When this happens, our redemption, our salvation, will be complete. Just as God made the

whole man and the whole man fell, so the whole man will be redeemed.

1 Corinthians 15:52-58; 1 Thessalonians 4:13, 14
The bodies of Christians who have died ("them who are asleep") will be raised from the dead when Christ comes back again.

1 Corinthians 15:51, 52; 1 Thessalonians 4:13-18
These verses show us that those Christians still alive when Christ comes back will not go through death. Their bodies will be changed in a twinkling of an eye—as fast as it takes to wink. They will pass immediately from this present life to full glorification.

Philippians 3:20, 21; 1 John 3:2
The glorified bodies of all Christians (whether they have died and have been raised again or have been changed in a twinkling of an eye) will be like Christ's body after His resurrection.

John 20:26
After His resurrection, Christ's body could pass through closed doors. After our glorification we will be able to do the same.

Luke 24:36-43
After His resurrection Christ could and did eat. After our glorification we will be able to do the same.

John 20:27, 28
The conclusion of each of the four Gospels and the beginning of Acts tell us what a wonderful body Christ had after His resurrection. But it is clear from verse 27 and others that this was not a new body that Christ had after His resurrection, but the same body that He had before His death and at His death. After our glorification, we will have the same bodies as we have now, but glorified. They will be changed bodies, glorified bodies, but the same bodies.

Things of the Future

THE EXTERNAL WORLD AND THE PEOPLE OF GOD

In this series of Bible studies, we have considered three large sections: "God," "God's Dealing with Man," and "Salvation." Now we will finish with a short section of two studies on "Things of the Future." Of course, what we have already studied of the Christian's glorification at death and at the resurrection is also future for us.

In this chapter we will look at the external world and the people of God.

Luke 17:26-30; 18:8

The world is not going to get better and better. The Christian's hope is not the gradual betterment of the world, but that Christ is coming back again.

Acts 1:10, 11; Mark 13:26; 1 Corinthians 15:23; Philippians 3:20, 21; 1 Thessalonians 1:10; 2:19; 3:13; 4:14, 16, 17; 2 Thessalonians 1:7; 1 Timothy 6:14; Titus 2:12, 13; 2 Peter 3:3-14; Revelation 1:7, 8

The fact of Christ's coming again is clearly stated. History is going someplace!

Acts 1:6-9; Matthew 24:36; 25:13; Mark 13:32, 33; Luke 12:35-40
The time of Christ's return is not given. These verses teach us not
to set times, saying we know when He is coming. On the other
hand, they tell us that Christ may come at any time. The Christian
should be constantly awaiting Him. The command is to "watch."

1 Thessalonians 3:13; 4:13-17
True Christians, those who have put their faith in Christ as Savior,
shall be caught up to meet Christ in the air and then come with
Him. It is at this time that the bodies of Christians who have died
will be raised from the dead and that living Christians will be glorified in a twinkling of an eye.

Matthew 24:36-44; Luke 17:26-30, 34-36; 21:36; Isaiah 26:19-21
Noah was out of danger in the ark before the flood came. Lot was
safe before the destruction of Sodom began. It would seem that
in the same way, true Christians will be taken out of danger
before God's wrath is poured out upon the earth. Some Christians
will be sleeping when they are taken, some will be awake. But all
true Christians will be taken. The unsaved will be left.

Matthew 25:1-13
In this parable the Lord shows that not even all of those who are
church members will be taken. Church members who have not
put their personal faith in Christ as their Savior will be left.

2 Thessalonians 2:1-12; Revelation 13:1-18
Before Christ's coming visibly and in glory with His saints, there
will be a period of great apostasy with a dictator, called "the
Antichrist," ruling the world. He is completely opposite and
opposed to Christ, completely subservient to Satan, the "dragon."
He will control governmental and economic life and will be wor-
shiped as God.

Revelation 6:1-17; 8:7—9:21; 11:13, 14; 15:1
God's wrath is poured out upon the earth during this period.

Revelation 16:13-16; 19:11-21
Here Christ comes visibly and in glory. He overthrows the assem-
bled might of the world organized against Him by the Antichrist
and Satan. This is the battle of Armageddon. This is not just a
great war between nations; it is the final confrontation between
the world's might under Antichrist and Satan, and Christ and the

glorified Christians. Armageddon is the plain of Megiddo in Palestine.

Revelation 20:1-6; Romans 8:18-23; Isaiah 11:1-10

The devil is shut up, and Christ rules the earth for a thousand years. The bodies of all true Christians will have been redeemed and glorified. Then the curse that God put upon the earth (Genesis 3:17, 18) because of man's sin will be removed. The world will, during this period, then be normal again—that is, as God made it.

Revelation 20:6; Luke 19:11-27

The Christians (servants) will reign with Christ during this period. Apparently our place of service in that time will be conditioned by our faithfulness in this present time.

Romans 11:25-29; Isaiah 11:10–12:6; Jeremiah 30:7-11; Zechariah 12:8-10; 13:6; 14:16-21

When Christ comes back in glory, the Jews will see Him as the true Messiah whom they, as a nation, rejected; and they will believe on Him.

Revelation 20:7-15

At the end of the thousand years, Satan will be loosed. There will be a final revolt against Christ, and the judgment of the lost will take place.

Revelation 21:1—22:5

There will be a new heaven, a new earth, and a heavenly city. It is definite, and so this passage can state the size of the heavenly city, that from which it is constructed, that from which its foundations, gates, and streets are made. It is an objective reality. It is eternal—forever and ever, without end.

> *When we've been there ten thousand years,*
> *Bright shining as the sun,*
> *We've no less days to sing God's praise,*
> *Than when we first begun.*

THE LOST

We have studied the present and future of those who have accepted God's gift of salvation by receiving Christ as Savior. This final study is the other side.

Revelation 19:20
This describes the end of the Antichrist and also of the false religious head who led in the worship of him.

Revelation 20:10
Originally created as the angel Lucifer ("son of the morning"), Satan revolted against God. This is his end.

Jude 6; 2 Peter 2:4; 1 Corinthians 6:3; Matthew 8:28, 29
This is the end of the angels who followed Satan in his revolt.

Romans 2:5, 6; 2 Thessalonians 1:4-9
There is a day of judgment for men and women who follow Satan in his revolt.

Daniel 12:2; John 5:28, 29; Acts 24:15
There will be a future physical resurrection of the lost.

Revelation 20:5, 6
The physical resurrection of the lost takes place a thousand years

after the physical resurrection of the Christians. All Christians are raised in the first resurrection, and they need not fear the "second death," the condemnation of the final judgment. Either a person must be twice-born (natural birth and the new birth when he takes Christ as Savior), or he must die twice (the natural death and eternal judgment).

John 8:44; Matthew 25:41, 46; Revelation 20:11-15
The end of the lost is the same as that of the devil and the angels who follow him. As the complete man (body and soul) of those who put their faith in Christ is redeemed, so the complete man (body and soul) of those who do not accept God's gift of salvation is judged. Hell is prepared for the devil and his angels, and the result of following him is to end up in the same place.

Matthew 3:12; 5:22; 8:12; 13:42, 50; 22:13; 25:30; Mark 9:43-48; 2 Peter 2:17; 3:7; Revelation 19:20; 20:15
In these and many other verses the Bible speaks of this place. Notice how much of this is given by Christ Himself, the One who came and died so that people might escape this by accepting Him as Savior.

Luke 12:48
There are degrees of judgment. As there is a believers' judgment, there are also degrees of judgment of the lost. There is a balancing of the books on both sides of the chasm.

Matthew 25:41, 46; 18:8; 2 Thessalonians 1:9; Jude 13; Revelation 20:10
The same words are used in the original Greek for the eternal quality of the future of the lost as are used for the eternal quality of the future of the redeemed. The two stand parallel.

In concluding this sober study, what should be in our minds?

Romans 5:8, 9; Ephesians 2:1-9; 1 Thessalonians 1:10
If we are Christians, remember that this is what we have been saved from by the death of Christ on Calvary. He suffered there infinitely, so that we might not be separated from God everlastingly.

Matthew 28:19, 20; Romans 10:13-15; Revelation 22:17
If we are Christians, in the light of this study we should give our-

selves to the task that Christ has given to the Church in this age—
telling others the content of the gospel.

Matthew 11:28-30

If you have not yet taken Christ as your Savior, if you are not a
Christian, the triune God invites you to come and accept God's
free gift of salvation by accepting Christ as Savior.

John 3:36

If you are not a Christian, you are here told that the judgment of
God is upon you. But this same verse tells you as clearly as can
be put into human language that there is only one thing necessary
to have that other everlasting, eternal life, immediately and without end.

PART

TWO

———

Two Contents,
Two Realities

PUBLISHER'S FOREWORD

For Dr. Francis Schaeffer the study of the Bible could never be separated from life as a whole. The Bible, Schaeffer stressed, is *truth*—not just truth in a narrow "religious" sense, but absolute truth that touches every area of human life.

For this reason we have included the following four brief chapters from the booklet *Two Contents, Two Realities*[1] along with the preceding basic Bible studies. On the one hand, the foregoing studies present a clear introduction to the foundational truths of God's Word. But beyond this, the following chapters stress the importance of living these truths out day-by-day, in the marketplace of modern life.

The title—*Two Contents, Two Realities*—provides the outline for the central themes of the booklet. "Two contents" refers first to the content of sound doctrine, founded on the absolutes of the Bible as these are carried out in the "practice of truth." The second content refers to facing the honest questions of our generation, and responding with the honest answers that are available in the Bible alone.

But as Schaeffer knew so clearly from his own experience, it is not enough simply to know sound doctrine and to know the right

answers. If we truly are Christians, there must also be a corresponding reality—the reality, first, of a moment-by-moment walk
with Christ, and the reality, second, of beauty in our relationships
with one another.

Having completed the foregoing Bible studies, then, I would
encourage you to read and reflect on the following chapters and to
discover the content and reality of God's Word lived out across the
whole spectrum of life. For, as Schaeffer concludes the booklet,
"when there are the two contents and the two realities, we will begin
to see something profound happen in our generation."

For those who are interested in reading further material by Dr.
Francis A Schaeffer, the following titles are recommended:

How Should We Then Live? (available from Crossway Books,
Wheaton, Illinois 60187) presents a penetrating Christian critique
of western culture from the time of Christ.

The *Francis A. Schaeffer Trilogy* (Crossway Books) includes
Schaeffer's three foundational books: *The God Who Is There*,
Escape from Reason, and *He Is There and He Is Not Silent*.

True Spirituality (available from Tyndale House, Wheaton,
Illinois 60189) provides a depth of insight into what it means to live
out the Christian life with reality.

Lastly, all of Schaeffer's twenty-two books are available in *The
Complete Works of Francis A. Schaeffer* (Crossway Books).

Lane T. Dennis,
President
Crossway Books

SOUND DOCTRINE

There are four things that I think are absolutely necessary if we as Christians are going to meet the need of our age and the overwhelming pressure we are increasingly facing. They are two contents and two realities:

The First Content: Sound Doctrine
The Second Content: Honest Answers to Honest Questions
The First Reality: True Spirituality
The Second Reality: The Beauty of Human Relationships

Clear Doctrinal Content

The first content is clear doctrinal content concerning the central elements of Christianity. There is no use talking about meeting the threat of the coming time or fulfilling our calling [at the close] of the twentieth century unless we consciously help each other to have a clear doctrinal position. We must have the courage to make no compromise with liberal theology and especially neo-orthodox, existential theology.

Christianity is a specific body of truth; it is a system, and we must not be ashamed of the word *system*. There is truth, and we must hold that truth. There will be borderline things in which we have differences among ourselves, but on the central issues there must be no compromise.

Evangelicals can fall into something that really is not very far from existential theology without knowing it. One form of such "evangelical existentialism" is the attitude, if not the words, "Don't ask questions, just believe." This sort of attitude was always wrong, but it is doubly wrong today when we are surrounded with a monolithic consensus that divides reason from nonreason and always puts religious things in the area of nonreason. We must call each other away from this idea. It is not more spiritual to believe without asking questions. It is not more biblical. It is less biblical, and eventually it will be less spiritual, because the whole man will not be involved. We must be absolutely determined not to fall into the trap of saying or implying, "Don't ask questions, just believe." It must be the whole man who comes to understand that the gospel is truth and believes because he is convinced on the basis of good and sufficient reason that it is truth.

Moreover, we must be very careful to emphasize content in our messages. How much content will depend upon the people with whom we are working. In a university setting, the content will be slightly different than in a situation where people are not as educated. Nevertheless, whether we work with a man or woman who is not as educated or whether we work with an intellectual, in all instances the gospel we preach must be rich in content. Certainly, we must be very careful not to fall into the cheap solution (which seems so fascinating at first) of just moving people to make decisions without their really knowing what they are making a decision about. We in L'Abri have had people come to us who have "accepted Christ as Savior" but are not even sure that God exists. They have never been confronted with the question of the existence of God.

The acceptance of Christ as Savior was a thing abstracted. It had an insufficient content. In reality, it was just another kind of trip.

Likewise, in a Christian school or college we can try just to religiously move the students on the basis of something apart from the intellect, separated from the academic disciplines and the whole of study. We must say no to this.

What we need to do is to understand our age to be an age of very subtle religious and political manipulation, manipulation by cool communication, communication without content. And as we see all these things, we must lean against them. We have a message of content; there is a system to Christianity. It is not *only* a system, true enough; it is not a dead scholasticism, true enough; but it *is* a system in that the person who accepts Christ as his Savior must do so in the midst of the understanding that prior to the creation of the world a personal God on the high level of Trinity existed. And if they "accept Christ as their Savior" and do not understand that God exists as an infinite-personal God, and do not understand that man has been made in the image of God and has value, and do not understand that man's dilemma is not metaphysical because he is small but moral because man revolted against God in a space-time Fall, in all probability they are not saved. If we "evangelize" by asking for such "acceptance of Christ as Savior," all we have done is to guarantee they will soon drift away and become harder to reach than ever. Not everybody must know everything—nobody knows everything; if we waited to be saved until we knew everything, nobody would ever be saved—but that is a very different thing from deliberately or thoughtlessly diminishing the content.

The Absolutes of the Bible

Another way to fall into an "evangelical existentialism" is to treat the first half of Genesis the way the existential theologian treats the whole Bible. The first half of Genesis is history, space-time history, the Fall is a space-time Fall, or we have no knowledge of what Jesus came to die for, and we have no way to understand that God is really a good God. Our whole answer to evil rests upon the historic, space-time Fall. There was a time before man revolted against God. The internal evidence of Genesis and the external evidences (given in the New Testament by the way the New Testament speaks of the first half of Genesis) show that the first half of Genesis is really meant to be space-time history—that is, space and time, the warp and woof of history.

In relationship to this is the danger of diminishing the content of the gospel in a reverse fashion. Bible-believing Christians who stand against the liberal theologian when he would say there are no absolutes in the Bible can make the opposite mistake by adding other elements as though they were equally absolute. In other words, the absolutes of the Word of God can be destroyed in both directions. That is, the liberal theologian can say, "After all, there is no such thing as an absolute, and specifically the Bible does not give absolutes," or the evangelical can reach over into the middle-class standards and say, "These standards are equal to the absolutes of the Word of God."

The obvious illustration is how the church treats the counterculture person or a person dressed in a different way. Young people come to us at L'Abri from the ends of the earth, become Christians, and go home and then try to find a Bible-believing church that will accept them without all the change of life-style. I do not mean they try to retain a drug life or a promiscuous sex life that would be against the Word of God. I mean, for example, the way they dress or talk. It is one of my greatest sorrows that the evangelical church often will not accept the person with his life-style unless it fits into the middle-class norm in that particular geographical location. And unhappily we often do not realize what we have done when we do this. It is not only a lack of love. We have destroyed the absolutes of the Word of God by making something else equal to God's absolutes.

If you ask me why the evangelical church has so often been

weak in the question of race in the past, I think it was the same.[2]
We were surrounded by a culture that had racial prejudices and that
did not look at all men as equal, and we allowed this to infiltrate the
church. We made taboos apart from and even against the Word of
God, and we held them to be equal with the absolutes of the Bible.
But to exalt a cultural norm to an absolute is even more destructive
today because we are surrounded by a totally relativistic society. As
we make other things equal to the absolutes of the Word of God, it
may not be more sinful in the sight of God than it was in the past,
but it is more destructive. Consequently, when we talk about content, we are talking about something very practical indeed. We must
have a strong, strong doctrinal content.

The Practice of Truth

And as we have a strong doctrinal content, we must practice the
content, practice the truth we say we believe. We must exhibit to our
own children and to the watching world that we take truth seriously.
It will not do in a relativistic age to say that we believe in truth and
fail to *practice that truth* in places where it may be observed and
where it is costly. We, as Christians, say we believe that truth exists.
We say we have truth from the Bible. And we say we can give that
truth to other men in propositional, verbalized form and they may
have that truth. This is exactly what the gospel claims, and this is
what we claim. But then we are surrounded by a relativistic age. Do
you think for a moment we will have credibility if we say we believe
the truth and yet do *not practice the truth in religious matters*? If
we do not do this, we cannot expect for a moment that the tough-
minded, twentieth-century young person (including our own young
people) will take us seriously when we say, "here is truth" when
they are surrounded by a totally monolithic consensus that truth
does not exist.

Consider an example in the academic world. One girl who was
teaching in one of the major universities of Britain was a real

Christian and very bright. She was teaching in a sociology depart-
ment whose head was a behaviorist, and he told her she had to
teach in the framework of behaviorism or lose her post. Suddenly
she was confronted with the question of the practice of truth. She
said no, she could not teach behaviorism, and she lost her post.
This is what I mean by practicing truth when it is costly. And this
will come in many, many places and in many, many ways. It will
come in the area of sexual life forms, being surrounded by per-
missive sexualists and asexuality. We must be careful by the grace
of God to practice what we say the Bible teaches—the one-man,
one-woman relationship—or we are destroying the truth that we
say we believe. And this practicing will include church discipline
where it is necessary.

But nowhere is practicing the truth more important than in the
area of religious cooperation. If I say that Christianity is really eternal truth, and the liberal theologian is wrong—so wrong that he is
teaching that which is contrary to the Word of God—and then on
any basis (including for the sake of evangelism) I am willing pub-
licly to act as though that man's religious position is the same as
my own, I have destroyed the practice of truth that my generation
can *expect* from me and that it will *demand* of me if I am to have
credibility. How will we have *credibility* in a relativistic age if we
practice religious cooperation with men who in their books and lec-
tures make very plain that they believe nothing (or practically nothing) of the content set forth in Scripture?

Incidentally, almost certainly if we have a latitudinarianism in
religious cooperation, the next generation will have a latitudinarianism in doctrine, and specifically a weakness toward the Bible. We
are seeing this happen in parts of evangelicalism as well. We must
have the courage to take a clear position.[3]

But let us beware. We certainly must not take every one of our
small secondary distinctives and elevate them to be the point where
we refuse to have fellowship on any level with those who do not

hold them. It is the central things of the Word of God that make Christianity Christianity. These we must hold tenaciously, and, even when it is costly for us and even when we must cry, we must maintain that there is not only an antithesis of truth, but an antithesis that is observable in practice. Out of a loyalty to the infinite-personal God who is there and who has spoken in Scripture, and out of compassion for our own young people and others, we who are evangelicals dare not take a halfway position concerning truth or the practice of truth.

Thus, with regard to the first content there are three things to recognize: first, there must be a strong emphasis on content; second, there must be a strong emphasis on the propositional nature of the Bible, especially the early chapters of Genesis; and third, there must be a strong emphasis on the practice of truth. We can talk about methods, we can stir each other up, we can call each other to all kinds of action, but unless it is rooted in a strong Christian base in the area of content and the practice of truth, we build on sand and add to the confusion of our day.

CHAPTER

TWO

———

HONEST ANSWERS
TO HONEST QUESTIONS

The second content is that Christianity is truth, and we must give honest answers to honest questions. Christianity is truth, truth that God has told us; and if it is truth, it can answer questions.

Truth for Every Aspect of Life

There is no dichotomy in the Bible between the intellectual and cultural on the one hand and the spiritual on the other. But often there has been a strong Platonic emphasis in evangelicalism, a strong tendency to divide man into two parts—his spiritual nature and everything else. We must take that conception like a piece of baked clay, break it in our hands, and throw it away. We must consciously reject the Platonic element that has been added to Christianity. God made the whole man; the whole man is redeemed in Christ. And after we are Christians, the Lordship of Christ covers the whole man. That includes his so-called spiritual things and his intellectual, creative, and cultural things; it includes his law, his sociology, and psychology; it includes every single part and portion of a man and his being.

The Bible does not suggest that there is something distinct in man that is spiritual and that the rest of man is unrelated to the commands and norms of God. There is nothing in the Bible that would say, "Never mind the intellectual, never mind the cultural. We will follow the Bible in the spiritual realm, but we will take the intellectual and the creative and put them aside. They are not important."

If Christianity is truth as the Bible claims, it must touch every aspect of life. If I draw a pie and that pie comprises the whole of life, Christianity will touch every slice. In every sphere of our lives, Christ will be our Lord and the Bible will be our norm. We will stand under the Scripture. It is not that the "spiritual" is under Scripture while the intellectual and creative are free from it.

Consider the ministry of Paul. Paul went to the Jews, and what happened as he talked to them? They asked Paul questions, and he answered. He went to the non-Jews, the Gentiles, and they asked him questions, and he answered. He went into the marketplace, and there his ministry was a ministry of discussion, of giving honest answers to honest questions. He went to Mars Hill, and he gave honest answers to honest questions. There are three places in the Bible where Paul was speaking to the man without the Bible (that is, to the Gentiles) without the man with the Bible (the Jew) being present. The first was at Lystra, and his discussion there was cut short. Then we find him on Mars Hill where they asked questions, and Paul answered; this too was cut short. But one place, happily, where he was not cut short is in the first two chapters of the book of Romans. And there we find carried out exactly the same kind of "argumentation" that he began at Lystra and on Mars Hill.

Many Christians think that 1 Corinthians speaks against the use of the intellect. But it does not. What 1 Corinthians speaks against is a man's pretending to be autonomous, drawing from his own wisdom and his own knowledge without recourse to the revelation of the Word of God. It is a humanistic, rationalistic intellectualism—a wisdom that is generated from man himself as opposed to the teaching of the Scripture—that we must stand against with all our hearts. Paul was against the early gnosticism, which said a man could be saved on the basis of such knowledge. Paul did answer questions. He answered questions wherever they arose.

Consider the ministry of our Lord Jesus Himself. What was His ministry like? He was constantly answering questions. Of course they were different kinds of questions from those that arose in the Greek and Roman world, and therefore His discussion was different. But as far as His practice was concerned, He was a man who answered questions, this Jesus Christ, this Son of God, this second person of the Trinity, our Savior and our Lord. But someone will say, "Didn't He say that to be saved you have to be as a little child?" Of course He did. But did you ever see a little child who didn't ask questions? People who use this argument must never have listened to a little child or been one! My four children gave me a harder time with their endless flow of questions than university people ever have. Jesus did not mean that coming as a little child simply meant making an upper-story leap [of faith]. What Jesus was talking about is that the little child, when he has an adequate answer, accepts the answer. He has the simplicity of not having a built-in grid whereby, regardless of the validity of the answer, he rejects it. And that is what rationalistic man, humanistic man, does.

Answering the Questions of Our Generation

Christianity demands that we have enough compassion to learn the questions of our generation. The trouble with too many of us is that we want to be able to answer these questions instantly, as though we could take a funnel, put it in one ear and pour in the facts, and then go out and regurgitate them and win all the discussions. It cannot be. Answering questions is hard work. Can you answer all the questions? No, but you must try. Begin to listen with compassion. Ask what this man's questions really are and try to answer. And if you don't know the answer, try to go someplace or read and study to find the answer.

Not everybody is called to answer the questions of the intellectual, but when you go down to the shipyard worker you have a similar task. My second pastorate was with shipyard workers, and I tell you they have the same questions as the university man. They just do not articulate them the same way.

Answers are not salvation. Salvation is bowing and accepting God as Creator and Christ as Savior. I must bow twice to become a Christian. I must bow and acknowledge that I am not autonomous; I am a creature created by the Creator. And I must bow and acknowledge that I am a guilty sinner who needs the finished work of Christ for my salvation. And there must be the work of the Holy Spirit. Nonetheless, what I am talking about is our responsibility to have enough compassion to pray and do the hard work that is necessary to answer the honest questions. Of course, we are not to study only cultural and intellectual issues. We ought to study them and the Bible and in both ask for the help of the Holy Spirit.

It is not true that every intellectual question is a moral dodge. There are honest intellectual questions, and somebody must be able to answer them. Maybe not everybody in your church or your young people's society can answer them, but the church should be training men and women who can. Our theological seminaries should be committed to this too. It is part of what Christian education ought to be all about.

The Final Test of Truth
The Bible puts a tremendous emphasis on content with which the mind can deal. In 1 John we are told what we should do if a spirit or a prophet knocks on our door tonight. If a prophet or spirit knocks on your door, how do you know whether or not he is from

God? I have a great respect for the occult, especially after the things we have seen and fought and wrestled against in L'Abri. If a spirit comes, how do you judge him? Or if a prophet comes, how do you judge him? John says, "Beloved, believe not every spirit, but test the spirits whether they are of God; because many false prophets are gone out into the world. By this know ye the Spirit of God; every spirit that confesseth that Jesus Christ is come in the flesh is of God" (1 John 4:1, 2).

Now that is a very profound answer; it has two halves. First, it means Jesus had an eternal preexistence as the second person of the Trinity, and then it means He came in the flesh. When a prophet or a spirit comes to you, the test of whether he should be accepted or rejected is not the experience that the spirit or prophet gives you. Nor is it the strength of the emotion that the spirit or the prophet gives you. Nor is it any special outward manifestations that the spirit or the prophet may give you. The basis of accepting the spirit or prophet—*and the basis of Christian fellowship*—is Christian doctrine. There is no other final test. Satan can counterfeit, and he will.

I am not speaking against emotion in itself. Of course there should be emotion. I am saying that you cannot trust your emotions or the strength of your emotions or the boost your emotions give you when you stand in the presence of the spirit or the prophet. This does not prove for one moment whether he is from God or the devil, or whether your emotions are simply from within yourself. And the same is true with Christian fellowship. These are to be tested, says the Word of God, at the point at which the mind can work, and that is on the basis of Christian doctrine.

So there are two contents, the content of a clear doctrinal position and the content of honest answers to honest questions. I now want to talk about two realities.

TRUE SPIRITUALITY

The first reality is spiritual reality. Let us emphasize again as we have before: we believe with all our hearts that Christian truth can be presented in propositions, and that anybody who diminishes the concept of the propositionalness of the Word of God is playing into twentieth-century, non-Christian hands. But, and it is a great and strong *but*, the end of Christianity is not the repetition of mere propositions. Without the proper propositions you cannot have that which should follow. But after having the correct propositions, the end of the matter is to love God with all our hearts and souls and minds. The end of the matter, after we know about God in the revelation He has given in verbalized, propositional terms in the Scripture, is to be in relationship to Him. A dead, ugly orthodoxy with no real spiritual reality must be rejected as sub-Christian.

A Crisis of Spiritual Reality

Back in 1951 and 1952, I went through a very deep time in my own life. I had been a pastor for ten years and a missionary for another five, and I was connected with a group who stood very strongly for the truth of the Scriptures. But as I watched, it became clear to me that I saw very little spiritual reality. I had to ask why. I looked at myself as well and realized that my own spiritual reality was not as great as it had been immediately after my conversion. We were in Switzerland at that time, and I said to my wife, "I must really think this through."

I took about two months, and I walked in the mountains whenever it was clear. And when it was rainy, I walked back and forth in the hayloft over our chalet. I thought and wrestled and prayed, and I went all the way back to my agnosticism. I asked myself whether I had been right to stop being an agnostic and to become a Christian. I told my wife, if it didn't turn out right I was going to be honest and go back to America and put it all aside and do some other work.

Moment-by-moment Reality

I came to realize that indeed I had been right in becoming a Christian. But then I went on further and wrestled deeper and asked, "But then where is the spiritual reality, Lord, among most of that which calls itself orthodoxy?" And gradually I found something. I found something that I had not been taught, a simple thing but profound. I discovered the meaning of the work of Christ, the meaning of the blood of Christ, moment by moment in our lives after we are Christians—the moment-by-moment work of the whole Trinity in our lives because as Christians we are indwelt by the Holy Spirit. That is true spirituality.

I went out to Dakota, and I spoke at a Bible conference. The Lord used it, and there was a real moving of God in that place. I preached it back in Switzerland. And gradually it became the book *True Spirituality*. And I want to tell you with all my heart that I think we could have had all the intellectual answers in the world at L'Abri, but if it had not been for those battles in which God gave me some knowledge of some spiritual reality in those days, not just theoretically but, poor as it was, knowledge of a relationship with God moment by moment on the basis of the blood of Jesus Christ, I don't believe there ever would have been a L'Abri.

Do we minimize the intellectual? I have just pled for the intellectual. I have pled for the propositional. I have pled against doctrinal compromises, specifically at the point of the Word of God being less than propositional truth all the way back to the first verse of Genesis. But at the same time there must be spiritual reality.

Will it be perfect? No. I do not believe the Bible ever holds out to us that anybody is perfect in this life. But it can be real, and it must be shown in some poor way. I say *poor* because I am sure when we get to Heaven and look back, we will all see how poor it has been. And yet there must be some reality. There must be something real of the work of Christ in the moment-by-moment life, something real of the forgiveness of specific sin brought under the blood of Christ, something real in Christ's bearing His fruit through me through the indwelling of the Holy Spirit. These things must be there. There is nothing more ugly in all the world, nothing that more turns people aside, than a dead orthodoxy.

This, then, is the first reality, real spiritual reality.

THE BEAUTY OF HUMAN RELATIONSHIPS

The second reality is the beauty of human relationships. True Christianity produces beauty as well as truth, especially in the specific areas of human relationships. Read the New Testament carefully with this in mind; notice how often Jesus returns us to this theme, how often Paul speaks of it. We are to show something to the watching world on the basis of the human relationships we have with other people, not just other Christians.

Christians today are the people who understand who man is. Modern man is in a dilemma because he does not know that man is qualitatively different from non-man. We say man is different because he is made in the image of God. But we must not say man is made in the image of God unless we look to God and by God's grace treat every man with dignity. We stand against B. F. Skinner in his book *Beyond Freedom and Dignity*. But I dare not argue against Skinner's determinism if I then treat the men I meet day by day as less than really made in the image of God.

Beauty Among Non-Christians

I am talking first of all about non-Christians. The first commandment is to love the Lord our God with all our heart and soul and mind, and the second is to love our neighbor as ourselves. After Jesus commanded this, someone said, "Who is my neighbor?" And Jesus then told the story of the good Samaritan. He was not just talking about treating Christians well; he was talking about treating every man we meet well, every man whether he is in our social stratum or not, every man whether he speaks our language or not, every man whether he has the color of our skin or not. Every man is to be treated on the level of truly being made in the image of God, and thus there is to be a beauty of human relationships.

This attitude is to operate on all levels. I meet a man in a revolving door. How much time do I have with him? Maybe ten seconds. I am to treat him well. We look at him. We do not think consciously in every case that this man is made in the image of God, but, having ground into our bones and into our consciousness (as well as our doctrinal statement) that he is made in the image of God, we will treat him well in those ten seconds that we have.

We approach a red light. We have the same problem. Perhaps we will never see these other people at the intersection again, but we are to remember that they have dignity.

And when we come to the longer relationships—for example, the employer-employee relationship—we are to treat each person with dignity. The husband-and-wife relationship, the parent-and-child relationship, the political relationship, the economic relationship[4]—in every single relationship of life, to the extent to which I am in contact with a man or woman, sometimes shorter and sometimes longer, he or she is to be treated in such a way that—man or woman—if he or she is thinking at all, he or she will say, "Didn't he treat me well!"

What about the liberal theologian? Yes, we are to stand against his theology. We are to practice truth, and we are not to compromise.

We are to stand in antithesis to his theology. But even though we cannot cooperate with him in religious things, we are to treat the liberal theologian in such a way that we try from our side to bring our discussion into the circle of truly human relationships. Can we do these two things together in our own strength? No. But in the strength of the power of the Holy Spirit, it can be done. We can have the beauty of human relationships even when we must say no.

Beauty Among Christians

Now, if we are called upon to love our neighbor as ourselves when he is not a Christian, how much more—ten thousand times ten thousand times more—should there be beauty in the relationships between true Bible-believing Christians, something so beautiful that the world would be brought up short! We must hold our distinctives. Some of us are Baptists, some of us hold to infant baptism, some of us are Lutheran, and so on. But to true Bible-believing Christians across all the lines, in all the camps, I emphasize: if we do not show beauty in the way we treat each other, then in the eyes of the world and in the eyes of our own children, we are destroying the truth we proclaim.

Every big company, if it is going to build a huge plant, first makes a pilot plant in order to show that their plan will work. Every church, every mission, every Christian school, every Christian group, regardless of what sphere it is in, should be a pilot plant that the world can look at and see there a beauty of human relationships that stands in exact contrast to the awful ugliness of what modern men paint in their art, what they make with their sculpture, what they show in their cinema, and how they treat each other. Men should see in the church a bold alternative to the way modern men treat people as animals and machines. There should be something so different that they will listen, something so different it will commend the gospel to them.

Every group ought to be like that, and our relationships between our groups ought to be like that. Have they been? The answer all too often is no. We have something to ask the Lord to forgive us for. Evangelicals, we who are true Bible-believing Christians, must ask God to forgive us for the ugliness with which we have often treated each other when we are in different camps.

I am talking now about *beauty*, and I have chosen this word with care. I could call it *love*, but we have so demoted the word that it is often meaningless. So I use the word *beauty*. There should be beauty, observable beauty, for the world to see in the way all true Christians treat each other.

Orthodoxy of Doctrine and Community

We need two orthodoxies: first, an orthodoxy of doctrine and, second, an orthodoxy of community. Why was the early church able, within one century, to spread from the Indus River to Spain? Think of that: one century, India to Spain. When we read in Acts and in the epistles, we find a church that *had* and *practiced* both orthodoxies (doctrine and community), and this could be observed by the world. Thus, they commended the gospel to the world of that day, and the Holy Spirit was not grieved.

There is a tradition (it is not in the Bible) that the world said about the Christians in the early church, "Behold, how they love each other." As we read Acts and the epistles, we realize that these early Christians were really struggling for a practicing community. We realize that one of the marks of the early church was a real community, a community that reached down all the way to their care for each other in their material needs.

Have we exhibited this community in our evangelical churches? I have to say no—by and large, no. Our churches have often been two things—preaching points and activity generators. When a person really has desperate needs in the area of race, or economic matters, or psychological matters, does he naturally expect to find a supporting community in our evangelical churches? We must say with tears, many times no!

My favorite church in Acts and, I guess, in all of history is the church at Antioch. I love the church at Antioch. I commend to you to read again about it. It was a place where something new happened: the great, proud Jews who despised the Gentiles (there was an anti-Gentilism among the Jews, just as so often, unhappily, there has been anti-Semitism among Gentiles) came to a breakthrough. They could not be silent. They told their Gentile neighbors about the gospel, and suddenly, on the basis of the blood of Christ and the truth of the Word of God, the racial thing was solved. There were Jewish Christians and there were Gentile Christians, and they were one!

More than that, there was a total span of the social spectrum. We are not told specifically that there were slaves in the church of Antioch, but we know there were in other places, and there is no reason to think they were not in Antioch. We know by the record in Acts that there was no less a person in that church than Herod's foster brother. The man at the very peak of the social pyramid and the man at the bottom of the pile met together in the church of the Lord Jesus Christ, and they were one in a beauty of human relationships.

And I love it for another reason. There was a man called Niger in that church, and that means "black." More than likely, he was a black man. The church at Antioch on the basis of the blood of Christ encompassed the whole. There was a beauty that the Greek and the Roman world did not know—and the world looked. And then there was the preaching of the gospel. In one generation the church spread from the Indus River to Spain. If we want to touch our generation, we must be no less than this.

I would emphasize again that community reached all the way down into the realm of material possessions. There is no communism, as we today know the word *communism*, in the book of Acts. Peter made very plain to Ananias and Sapphira that their land was their own, and when they had sold their land they were masters of what they did with the money. No state or church law, no legalism, bound them. What existed in the early church was a love that was so overwhelming that they could not imagine in the church of the Lord Jesus having one man hungry and one man rich. When the Corinthian church fell into this, Paul was scathing in 1 Corinthians in writing against it.

Note, too, that deacons were appointed. Why? Because the church had found difficulty in caring for one another's material needs. Read James 2. James asks, "What are you doing preaching the gospel to a man and trying to have a good relationship with him spiritually if he needs shoes and you do not give him shoes?" Here is another place where the awful Platonic element in the evangelical church has been so dominant and so deadly. It has been considered spiritual to give for missions, but not equally spiritual to give when my brother needs shoes. That is never found in the Word of God. Of course, the early church gave to missions; at times they gave money so Paul did not have to make tents. But Paul makes no distinction between collections for missions and collections for material needs, as if one were spiritual and the other not. For the most part when Paul spoke of financial matters, he did so because there was a group of Christians somewhere who had a material need, and Paul then called upon other churches to help.

Moreover, it was not only in the local church that the Christians cared for each other's needs; they did so at great distances. The church of Macedonia, which was made up of Gentile Christians, when they heard that the Jewish Christians, the Jews whom they would previously have despised, had material need, took an offering and sent it with care hundreds of miles in order that the Jewish Christians might eat.

So, there must be two orthodoxies: the orthodoxy of doctrine and the orthodoxy of community. And both orthodoxies must be practiced down into the warp and the woof of life where the Lordship of the Lord Jesus touches every area of our life.

Thus there are four requirements if we are to meet the needs of our generation. They are the two contents and then the two realities. [The first content is *Sound Doctrine*; the second content is *Honest Answers to Honest Questions*; the first reality is *True Spirituality*; and the second reality is *The Beauty of Human Relationships*.] And when there are the two contents and the two realities, we will begin to see something profound happen in our generation.

NOTES

1. Publisher's note: The text of *Two Contents, Two Realities* was first presented as a position paper by Francis Schaeffer for the International Congress on World Evangelization, Lausanne, Switzerland, July 1974. The text as it appears in this edition remains the same as used in Schaeffer's *Complete Works* except where edited slightly for clarity, as indicated by brackets in these three instances. The text has also been broken into chapters corresponding to the original sections, and new section headings have been added.

2. I deal with this weakness concerning the question of race in *How Should We Then Live?*

3. See Chapters 1 and 5 of *No Final Conflict*. Chapter 1 was a part of my talk given to the International Congress on World Evangelization in Lausanne. It is an integral unit with this position paper.

4. The necessity of a compassionate use of accumulated wealth is dealt with in *How Should We Then Live?*